Parliamentary Portions

Compiled by

Liz Blackman MP & Nick Palmer MP

Edited by

Philipa Coughlan

Parliamentary Portions

A Gourmet's Guide to the
New House of Commons

Including special dishes from the
Prime Minister,
Rt. Hon Tony Blair MP
and
Madam Speaker
Rt. Hon Betty Boothroyd MP

Politico's PUBLISHING

First published in Great Britain 1998
by Politico's Publishing
8 Artillery Row
London
SW1P 1RZ
England
Tel 0171 931 0090
Email politicos@artillery-row.demon.co.uk
Website http://www.politicos.co.uk

A catalogue record for this book is available from the British Library

ISBN 1902301064

Cover illustration by Hoby, David Haselhurst
Printed and bound in Great Britain by St Edmundsbury Press.
Typsetting by FSH. Cover Design by AdVantage.

Contents

"Government is like a big baby – an alimentary canal with a big appetite at one end and no responsibility at the other."

Ronald Reagan

"The healthy stomach is nothing if not conservative. Few radicals have good digestions."

Samuel Butler

Dedicated to the memory and inspiration of Margaret Jeffries

Biographical Portions

Parliamentary Portions has been compiled by Liz Blackman, MP (Erewash) and Nick Palmer, MP (Broxtowe) who are donating proceeds from the sale of the book to their favourite charities – Cancer Research and The Cats Protection League.

To make donations, or for further information about these charities contact:

Cancer Research Campaign
10 Cambridge Terrace
London
NW1 4JL
Tel 0171 224 1333

Cats Protection League
17 Kings Road
Horsham
West Sussex
RH13 5PN
Tel 01403 221900

Liz Blackman is a former teacher who swept to victory at the 1997 General Election over Conservative Angela Knight in the Derbyshire constituency of Erewash with a 9,135 majority. Her main specialist topics are education, local community issues and economic regeneration. Liz was chosen to sit on the highly influential Treasury Select Committee soon after the election, where she has held her own amongst a strong pro and sceptic Euro split membership. Liz has also fought to secure more equality for the East Midlands from the Lottery Grant Funding of projects. A high priority in her life are her two children, Neil and Anna. Liz's chosen charity Cancer Research is close to her heart.

Nick Palmer, although 90th on the 'hit-list' of possible target seats for Labour overturned the long-serving Conservative Sir Jim Lester with a 5,575 majority in Broxtowe, Nottinghamshire. Nick has maintained a high profile for animal welfare issues in

Westminster, and introduced suggested Bills on air gun restrictions and compensation for the RSPCA for keeping ill treated animals. He has continued his firm stance against the anti-hunting lobby. Nick's other interests mirror his previous career focus on industry and Europe. He has published books on the subject of war game designs. Nick's chosen charity, The Cats Protection League, reflects his life time membership of the organisation.

Philipa Coughlan works as Parliamentary Secretary to both MPs at Westminster. Whilst campaigning for the Labour Party against railway privatisation in 1993, she was struck by a car and left partially disabled. She previously worked with Nick Palmer as part of the Editorial Team of the internal Labour magazine, 'Grass Roots.' She lives in Sussex with husband Dominic, and two sons Nicholas and Sean.

Introduction

On 1st May 1997 Labour gained a 177 landslide majority over all other Parties. Labour finished a momentous night with 418 seats to the Conservatives' 165. The Liberal Democrats had their best result for half a century.

In the new Parliament there are 260 new Members of Parliament. Many are young, many have young children and nearly half of them are women.

Has this changed the culture of the Commons?

A diversity of cultures, backgrounds and interests are now to be found in the corridors of Westminster. Their views are being sought on many wide ranging issues.

In this unusual cookbook we see the diversity of the new Parliament at its best, with regional, individual and sometimes eccentric tastes. We also see how Westminster people feed not their minds but refuel their aching bodies. It's a hard job, but somebody's got to do it...

Foreword

by Raymond Blanc - Chef and Proprietor of 'Maison aux Quatre Saisons'

'As many historic decisions have been made over a fine meal and perhaps a few too many glasses of wine, it is delightful to see that the politicians of Britain actually pay enough attention to their food so as to be able to provide the odd recipe. A contented stomach lined with the naturally produced wonders of land and sea can only make for a clear mind and a swift view of the best option. I can hardly believe that there is only one drink recipe available from the present cabinet; please honoured members; moderation is fine!

In a country that 20 years ago could not provide a herb apart from parsley, or a lettuce apart from iceberg, leaps and bounds have been made. The next serious step, in my opinion, would be to subsidise organic farmers. Who makes these decisions?'

Raymond Blanc

Section One

Breakfasts *or* Early Day Motions

Breakfasts

MPs often have to spend late nights in the House of Commons contributing to debates or waiting for calls to vote on major issues. Although there are facilities to eat in most parts of the Palace of Westminster during the night, most MPs like to try and forget food and grab a few hours sleep. The next morning they wake, weary but famished and requiring a good breakfast.

They may then also feel able to submit an Early Day Motion. This unseemly titled offering is in fact an opportunity for any MP to offer a subject for possible debate within the Chamber of the House of Commons. Each day that the Commons is in session a number of Early Day Motions (EDMs) are tabled. MPs can express views on particular issues with the protection of Parliamentary privilege. They can also see how popular that view might be in the House of Commons generally by the number of MPs willing to support its discussion who agree to sign the EDM paper. Some very popular or controversial issues may then have to be taken up in longer debates.

In fact, EDMs are rarely debated on the floor of the House. They appear in the House of Commons Order Paper which is normally only read by Parliamentarians, journalists, lobbyists and insomniacs. EDMs were once memorably described as 'graffiti on the walls of Parliament', which is hardly surprising when MPs use them to congratulate their local football team on winning the Zenith Data Cup.

Bob Russell

Liberal Democrat Colchester

Bob has sent in an elegantly decorated All Day Breakfast recipe. As a former journalist no doubt he has sampled many an early feast before tackling a report and continues to require such hearty sustenance at Westminster. Bob has offered to provide a demonstration! Only MPs with a good stomach lining had better apply...

A Full English Breakfast – or perhaps 'The Full Monty'

Ingredients:

Small tin of baked beans (preferably Heinz, best tasting tomato sauce) two fresh free range eggs, two rashers of streaky bacon (English, unsalted), handful of small mushrooms, two (cold) boiled potatoes, one pork sausage, one tomato, half slice of white bread.

Instructions:

Open tin of beans and empty into small saucepan. Slice potatoes, disc shape, cut tomato in half. Heat fat in frying pan, then place potatoes, bacon, sausage, mushrooms and tomato in pan and cook to required standard, turning them with slice; remove and place on side plate and cover. Then break shells of eggs and carefully put eggs into pan without breaking yolks; also place slice of bread into pan. When eggs are fried to required condition, turn over fried bread and place eggs on this. Place saucepan of beans on second ring and warm to required temperature. Return other items of food from side plate to frying pan to reheat to required temperature.

Serving:

Place beans to one side of plate, and then remove other items from frying pan and carefully fill rest of plate. For garnish, a dash of HP brown sauce next to sausage and bacon; a sprinkling of pepper on egg yolks. Side plate: Slices of white toast (other half to the fried piece, plus another full slice) with Wilkins (Tiptree, Colchester) jam or marmalade. Drink: A mug of hot tea (preferably Tetley) two sugars (stirred from the left)...then enjoy!

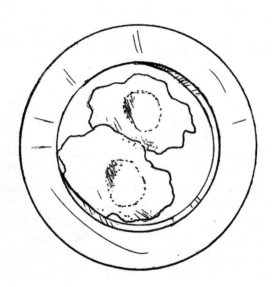

Michael Foster

Labour Hastings and Rye

For a rather special breakfast, Michael, a charming solicitor from the Sussex collection of new Southern MPs, has submitted the following.

Scrambled Eggs with Smoked Salmon

Ingredients:

4 eggs
2 tablespoons milk
Knob of butter
Salt and pepper
Slivers of smoked salmon

Method:

Break the eggs into a basin. Beat the eggs lightly, add the milk and seasoning. Melt the butter in a pan. Pour in the egg mixture and stir over a low heat until the eggs are just beginning to set. It is important to remove the eggs from the heat as they are just setting as the heat of the pan finishes the cooking. Add the slivers of smoked salmon and serve immediately with toasted bagels.

Valerie Davey

Labour Bristol West

Valerie, one of many teachers now in the Commons, who loves marmalade, has sent in her favourite Lemon Marmalade recipe. She says it is very simple, definitely needing a chopping block! Time and patience will be needed to cut up all the fruit. It is an adaptation of a Seville orange recipe handed on by a friend and Valerie also suggests trying Grapefruit and Stem Ginger as another combination.

Lemon Marmalade

Ingredients:

3-4 lbs of lemons
5 lbs of sugar
1 and a half pints of water

Method:

Put whole fruit in pressure cooker with water. Pressure cook at 15 lbs for about 10 mins. Cool – cut up fruit, discard pips. Keep juice. Put in preserving pan with sugar and boil till set (about 20 minutes) Makes 8 lbs marmalade (approx)

Jeffrey Donaldson

Ulster Unionist-Lagan Valley

Jeffrey, like so many members with constituencies in areas with strong regional traditions, has sent in something of the flavour of the place which he represents.

Ulster Soda Bread

Ingredients:

1lb/450 grams Wholemeal flour
8 oz/225 grams self-raising flour
1 dessertspoon of castor sugar
1 teaspoon salt
1 teaspoon baking soda/bicarbonate of soda
Approx 12–15 fl ozs /470 mls buttermilk

Method:

Put two flours into a mixing bowl. Add remaining dry ingredients and mix so as to incorporate and aerate. Lastly make a well in the centre and combine with enough buttermilk to make moist but firm dough. Turn out onto a floured surface and knead lightly. Form into a rounded shape and place onto a floured baking sheet. Using a knife, mark a cross pattern on top. Bake at 200°C/400°F for 40 minutes or until bread is brown and sounds hollow when tapped. Cool on a wire rack.

Tom Levitt

Labour-High Peak

One of the very traditional recipes for a breakfast dish has been sent in by Tom, although with a little added style and flavour that has made it his own…

Kedgeree

Ingredients:

1 portion of smoked haddock (smoked cod at a push) per person

1 standard mug of Basmati rice for three to four people

1 hard boiled egg per person

1 and a half tomatoes per person

Salt and pepper, fresh parsley for garnish

Method:

Boil the haddock in a minimum of water. You can put the eggs in with the haddock to boil them at the same time. Do not overdo the haddock but it should be tender and come apart with a firm squeeze when done.

My preferred way of boiling rice is as follows: Find a pan with a tight fitting lid, mix rice with a tablespoon of oil and some salt and then add double the amount of water as there is rice. Leave to stand for at least 20 minutes. Bring the rice to the boil. When the lid starts to rattle turn off the heat and leave it to stand. A good quality rice like Basmati will have absorbed all the water by this time without going gooey. (If you have time you can use the water that the haddock was boiled in for your rice. If you haven't got time, then add some tumeric to the rice before cooking to add a bit of colour). Chop the tomato and boiled eggs into small pieces. Mix the flaked haddock, rice, tomato and eggs and place in a well greased container. Put into the oven at Gas mark 5 for half an hour with a couple of knobs of butter on top. Serve with parsley garnish and hot bread with butter.

John McDonnell

Labour-Hayes and Harlington

John has submitted this most unusual, probably very unhealthy, but still quite tempting item that perhaps, as he said, can only loosely be given the status of a 'recipe'.

Sugar Sandwich

Method:

Take two slices of white bread. Smear with heavy dollop of Fussell's condensed milk. Shake over evenly a spoonful of white sugar per side of bread. For spectacular effect put both slices together and toast. (But not in the toaster or you will set the kitchen ablaze!)

Section Two

Starters/Appetisers, *or* Ten Minute Rule Bills

Starters/Appetisers or Ten Minute Rule Bills

The ability to stop and have a small snack or just a starter course is a pleasure within many cafeterias and restaurants at Westminster. The wonderful variety of homemade soup, served daily, which is both hearty, healthy and tasty (and cheap!) makes it perhaps the best soup kitchen in London! But a small snack to stop the grumbling tummy in the Chamber can always be found.

Opportunities for backbenchers to speak in the Chamber are sometimes few and far between. However, the Ten Minute Rule Bills are the exception. Their introduction is proposed by backbenchers at the beginning of public business on Tuesdays and Wednesdays, usually from the seventh week of a session (but not on Budget Day). It is a speech which is limited to ten minutes. If another backbencher opposes it, another ten minute speech is also permitted. Others in the House of Commons also have the right to say whether the Ten Minute Bill can be introduced at all. But they are popular in giving the opportunity for backbenchers to canvass ideas for future legislation. However, even when backbenchers get leave to introduce a Bill it will still face the many hurdles which Private Members Bills come up against in the Commons.

Ten Minute Rule Bills are an ideal way of promoting a cause and gaining a platform which may be reported in the media, particularly as the debates take place just after Question Time.

Steve Webb

Liberal-Democrat Northavon

Steve, whose profession and political thinking revolves around social policy, probably with concerns about the family, has thought up a recipe which even the kids can 'help' make. The finished product can be eaten straight away or cold at a picnic with the kids, or a cocktail party with the adults.

Children's Chicken and Apple Balls

Ingredients:

3 chicken breasts

1 eating apple (peeled)

1 handful of raisins and sultanas

1 large squeeze of lemon juice

1 small onion finely chopped

1 small garlic clove (peeled and finely chopped)

1 egg (beaten)

pinch of oregano, plain flour, oil

Method:

Chop chicken and apple in the processor. Mix in the raisins, sultanas, lemon juice, onion and garlic and use enough egg to bind the ingredients together. Form the mix into balls and roll in the flour. Heat the oil in a frying pan and fry the balls until they are golden brown and cooked through.

Stephen Twigg

Labour-Enfield Southgate

This young former Labour researcher found instant fame on General Election night in 1997 when he dramatically beat Defence Secretary and potential party Leader, Michael Portillo. The result remains one of the enduring images of the night, but here Stephen has given us a simple, down to earth recipe that he claims tastes absolutely magnificent.

Leek and Potato Soup

3-4 medium sized potatoes
3-4 leeks, use only the white part
100g butter
2 pints of chicken or vegetable stock
Half a cup of milk or cream
Pepper & salt

Method:

Cut the leeks into slices and fry them in the melted butter in a pot. Make sure that neither the butter or the leeks brown. Add the potatoes and a touch of salt. Let it simmer under a lid for a few minutes on medium heat. Add the first pint of stock and let it boil for around 35-40 minutes. Take it off the heat and blend it. Put it back on the heat and add the second pint of stock. Add half a cup of milk or cream and heat to the boiling point. Taste with salt and white pepper.

James Gray

Conservative-Wiltshire North

James has sent in a local Dairy Farm recipe, that is probably well known to all of us, but here has the enhancement of a definite regional flavour, that includes many ingredients specifically from local producers.

Wiltshire Rarebit – from the Wiltshire Tracklement Company Ltd

Thinly slice or grate good Wiltshire Cheddar or Double Gloucester to cover the bottom of a thick saucepan. Thinly spread with Urchfont Original Mustard then cover with Wadworth 6X or Old Timer beer. Melt over a slow heat.

Roughly mash 4 or 5 potatoes, boiled in their skins, in a fire proof dish then pour the melted cheese and beer over them. Finish under the grill with finely cut strips of Sandridge Farm streaky bacon laid over the top.

Mark Oaten

Liberal Democrat-Winchester

With two General Elections under his belt, it hardly seems surprising that the recipe sent in via his wife Belinda, is in fact from Mark's mother-in-law, and hasn't had much opportunity to be eaten over the past year. However, that may alter now his first majority of two votes has been somewhat increased.

Parsnip Soup
Serves 6

Ingredients:

40 g English butter
1 large onion
1 and a half pounds parsnips
2 and a quarter pints chicken stock
1 level teaspoon curry powder
Half a level teaspoon cumin
5 fl oz single cream

Method:

Heat butter and fry onion and parsnips together for about 3 minutes. Stir in curry powder and ground cumin and fry for a further 2 minutes. Add stock. Bring to the boil, lower heat and simmer for 45 minutes until tender. Blend in liquidiser until puréed. Return to the pan, adjust seasoning and add cream. Reheat without boiling. Serve.

Lembit Öpik

Liberal Democrat-Montgomeryshire

During the year Lembit was very seriously injured in an accident, but still bravely sent in his contribution from hospital. He says it is an old student favourite of his and, believe it or not, does actually taste very good. It also has the added advantage of being very quick to cook, and can be made with ingredients that almost everyone will have lying around somewhere! Lembit quickly adds that he does cook normal food too, though he admits that it doesn't happen very often...

Question Time Late Night TV Snack

Begin cooking at the start of the music and it should be ready by the end of David Dimbleby's introductory comments...

Ingredients:

Three Quarters of a pound of matured cheese, grated

half a pint of milk

1 tablespoon of flour

mixed herbs

as much garlic sauce as you can stand

Pringles – Cheese and Chive flavour for dipping

Method:

Stir all the ingredients together over a gentle heat until all melted together. Then eat!

Warning:

It doesn't taste good cold! Anything left over can be used as a putty substitute around your windows.

Des Browne

Labour-Kilmarnock & Loudon

An advocate from Scotland, Des has sent in a flavoursome fish treat from North of the Border.

Potted Herrings

Ingredients:

8 Herring (Ask your fishmonger to clean and fillet the fish)

Quarter pint water

Half a pint non brewed condiment, or white vinegar

One or two Bay leaves

A large onion

1 teaspoon of black peppercorns

Half teaspoon of pickling spice

Salt and pepper to taste

Optional – 1 Soupspoonful of granulated sugar

Method:

Set the oven to 180 degrees (moderate)

Use a lidded Pyrex dish big enough to take the rolled up fish, but small enough to hold the rolls of fish together. Wash the fish, then spread on a piece of greaseproof paper and salt them well. Roll them up, and place them in the Pyrex dish. Tuck the bay leaves in between the fish. Sprinkle the spices over the fish, and place the finely chopped onion on top of and around the fish. Mix the vinegar and water. I like to add a little sugar, but this is a matter of taste. Pour the mixture over the fish. Bake the fish for about 30-40 minutes. Allow to cool in dish.

Serve cold with salad and buttered brown soda bread.

Ross Cranston

Labour-Dudley North

Ross has in the past attended the University of Queensland and Harvard Law School, which perhaps gives us a clue to his liking for this particular recipe.

Pumpkin Soup

The required stock is made with one chicken stock cube, 1 pint of water and a piled tablespoon of chopped onion, which has been sweated until soft with a few specks of butter in a small covered saucepan. As soon as the onion has softened, remove the lid and continue shaking onion held up high over heat until the buttery fluid steams off. Have 1lb nett weight of firm boiled pumpkin ready and combine pumpkin, onion and lukewarm stock and put through the blender. Gradually heat the puree tasting for salt and pepper. Just before serving, stir in a piled tablespoon of thick cream through the soup. This may be skipped for health reasons. Serve with a small float of cream lightly sprinkled with finely chopped chives. Once again, you can skip the cream.

Note: You don't have to make the stock ahead. Just bung in the cube with warm water into the blender after the onion and pumpkin. Also the amount of pumpkin you can use is very flexible so long as the result is good and thick.

Owen Paterson

Conservative–Shropshire North

Owen claims that cooking is not one of his strong points, but has nevertheless forwarded quite a tasty little dish, even if it leaves a mess behind in the kitchen!

Garlic Eggs

Break an egg into a ramekin dish. Add a chopped garlic clove, salt, pepper and a dollop of cream. Put in a hot oven for about five minutes, or until you remember to take it out. Eat quickly, before the complaints about the smell of garlic become too insistent. Soak the ramekin for at least three days to get the burnt egg off the sides!!

Claire

Curtis-Thomas

Labour-Crosby

Claire has sent in a recipe for a 'great soup – smooth, smooth texture, subtle taste and beautiful colour'.

Nettle Soup

Ingredients:

1.5 pounds/750g Fresh young nettles
(available from March-April)
Wear gloves! Also wellingtons when collecting,
avoid busy roads, and guard all good locations jealously)

Half a pound/250g Onions – chopped
(Any variety, cheap and cheerful are fine)

2 tablespoons – Olive Oil

1 pint/0.6 litre Vegetable stock

Method:

Chop nettles roughly, including stem. Sauté onions in oil until translucent. Add nettles and continue to sauté until reduced. Add the vegetable stock and simmer all ingredients for 25 minutes. Blend and add 2 or 3 dollops of yoghurt and a smudge of black pepper and salt to taste.

Claire says of the end result: 'You have just arrived in Paradise. Adopt a conservative approach – do not share with friends!'

Harold Best

Labour-Leeds North West

As submitted to Harold by one of his constituents. We wonder whether any of the MP's surgeries take place in the allotments as well?

Ash Road Allotments Salad

Take 500 grams of leeks (the white part only) and clean them thoroughly. Thin ones are best, in which case leave them whole; if they are fat, cut them in half lengthways, leaving the halves joined at the base. Cook in boiling salted water until they are just tender, drain, cool and drain again, getting out as much water as possible. Cut into 3 cm lengths.

Cook 125 grams bacon very well, cool and cut into strips. Skin, deseed and dice 250 grams of tomatoes. Make a vinaigrette dressing: mix together salt and pepper, 1 tablespoon of wine vinegar and 3-5 tablespoons of olive oil according to taste.

Arrange the leeks on a serving dish, scatter over the bacon and tomatoes, and pour the well-mixed dressing over. Serve with good bread.

Vegetarians may substitute quartered hard-boiled eggs for the bacon.

Dr Jenny Tonge

Liberal Democrat-Richmond Park

Jenny claims her real favourite recipe is baked beans on toast! However, she has sought out her husband Keith on his allotment to supply this tasty soup which, she says, uses up his root crops!

Manor Road Allotment Beetroot Soup

Ingredients

1 lb Beetroot, 1 onion, 1 carrot, 1 turnip, 1 large potato, 1 stick of celery

2 pints of strong, meaty stock, 1 bay leaf, chopped parsley

1 tablesp tomato puree, 1 level tsp sugar, 1 tablesp lemon juice

5 fluid ounces of soured cream

Chopped mint, chives and spring onions to garnish

Salt and pepper to taste

Method:

Peel vegetables and set aside 4 ounces of beetroot. Dice and thinly slice all vegetables. Put all vegetables (except reserved beetroot) into a large pan with stock, herbs and salt and pepper. Simmer for 30 minutes. Mix tomato puree, sugar and lemon juice and add to soup. Simmer for a further 30 minutes or until vegetables are tender.

Ten minutes before serving, add reserved beetroot to soup. Stir 4–5 tablespoons of soup into cream and gradually add this to soup, stirring all the time. Heat through thoroughly but do not allow to boil.

Serve garnished with chopped mint, chopped chives and spring onions.

This can be served cold over ice-cubes in the Summer.

Timothy Loughton

Conservative-Worthing East and Shoreham

Tim is obviously picturing a balmy summer evening by the Sussex coast with this recipe in mind. He says: 'A quick and simple appetiser to the typical barbeque, for your guests who are increasingly impatient with the sausages taking forever to cook. It gives the cook something to do whilst waiting for the meat after all the problem of getting the barbeque lit in the first place, then serving guests before all traces of natural light have disappeared, and the midges attack in force!'

B. B. Q. Scallops

Method:

Using a small cast-iron pan, heat up some olive oil with some freshly crushed garlic, fresh herbs from the garden, lemon juice and a few drops of soy sauce. When the oil in the pan is sizzling put in the scallops for a few minutes until they have changed colour on both sides. Then fill the pan with generous amounts of cream together with a few splashes of white wine from the glass in your hand or something stronger if you prefer. Serve up to guests in small ramekin dishes with a teaspoon and they should wait with a little more patience for the main course to arrive.

Syd Rapson

Labour-Portsmouth North

A hint of the nearby sea here for Syd's recipe though with a touch of the continental! It's certainly quick!

Tiger Prawns

Lightly fry tiger prawns in garlic butter and serve on a green salad.

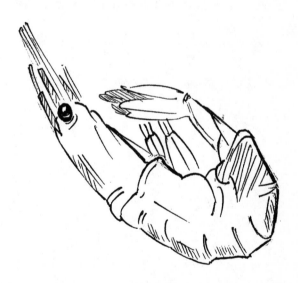

Martin Bell

Independent-Tatton

No collection of the new 1997 intake would be complete without something from the only independent MP in the House of Commons. The former TV news reporter was a familiar face on our screens as he travelled the war torn countries of the world but he entered a far more notorious conflict area when he was selected to stand as the 'anti-sleaze' candidate in sole opposition to former Conservative MP Neil Hamilton (and his wife Christine!). Martin says that his recipe for Sarajevo dandelion soup remains a closely guarded secret! But for a warm summer evening he recommends the following as a starter before the steaks, burgers and bangers or as a main dish with the potatoes.

Chicken portions cooked on the barbecue (jacket potatoes — cooked in the embers wrapped in foil) — with lashings of barbecue sauce.

Steve Ladyman

Labour-Thanet South

Steve, who studied at Liverpool Polytechnic, says that the bacon ribs in this recipe are commonly sold in the North West of England, especially around Merseyside, but elsewhere in the UK you might have to order them from your butcher. He insists that Bacon Spare ribs are the only choice – pork spare ribs do not work at all with this recipe!

Bacon Spare Ribs and Lentil Soup

Depending on your appetite take about 2 sheets of Bacon Spare Ribs and cut them between the ribs into more manageable sheets. Put the ribs in a large pan and cover with water and bring to the boil, then throw the water away, cover with fresh water bring to the boil again and then throw the water away again.

Then take: 1 large carrot and 1 large onion, both thinly sliced and 1 large potato finely diced and fry in about 60g of butter for 7-10 minutes. Then put them into the pan with the ribs. Add 150g split red lentils, 750ml of fresh milk, 500ml water and a vegetable stock cube; the ribs must be completely covered by liquid, if not add more water.

Bring to the boil and then lower the heat. Cover and simmer for at least one hour. The rib meat should be cooked thoroughly and quite soft, otherwise cook a little longer. Remove the ribs from the liquid and keep them warm until the soup is finished. Liquidise the soup with a blender. If the soup has reduced too much add more water and mix further with the blender. Then strain through a sieve. Reheat the soup and add a pinch of nutmeg, freshly ground pepper and salt to taste (be careful with the salt as bacon ribs are often salty and much of the salt will already be in the soup) If you wish stir in 200ml of fresh single cream immediately before serving. Pour the soup into warm bowls.

The ribs have to be eaten with fingers and dipped in the soup as you eat them so this is not a dish for a sophisticated dinner party! Everyone will get very, very messy!

Section Three

Speaker's Special

Madam Speaker

Betty Boothroyd

West Bromwich West

In all matters, the Speaker must remain fair and impartial, but controversy follows her here to the kitchen. For dished up in the Speaker's apartments do we dare to find a BANNED MEAT DISH? (Consultation with the Ministry of Agriculture, Food and Fisheries must surely follow)

However, like the wonderful lady herself the recipe remains traditional, well loved and warming.

Stewed Oxtail
Serves 4

Ingredients:

1 Oxtail – divided at the joints
1 large onion – sliced
3 carrots – diced
3-4 young turnips – diced
3 cloves, 1 blade of mace, quarter teaspoon allspice, bouquet garni (optional)
Seasoning
1 tablespn lemon juice

Method

Place oxtail in saucepan and cover with water. Boil for quarter of an hour. Drain to remove scum. Replace meat in pan, add vegetables, seasoning and spices and herbs if used. Cover with fresh water. Simmer until tender – approx 2 and a half hours. Add lemon juice. Serve on a hot dish with croutons or snippets of toast.

(Oxtail takes a long time to cook so it is well to cook it partially the day before. Another advantage of this is that it can be set in a bowl overnight, the grease will be solidified on top by the next morning and can then be skimmed off. This makes the stew less rich and much more digestible).

For something less controversial, she also suggests:

Roseanne's Lemon Chicken

Ingredients:

4 chicken breasts
Olive oil
Grated rind and juice of 2 lemons
1 onion, (finely chopped)
1 stick of celery (finely chopped)
Few sprigs of thyme
Salt and pepper
Half a pint of chicken stock
Watercress and lemon twists to garnish

Method:

Brush chicken breasts with olice oil and marinate for 3-4 hours in lemon rind and juice. Make chicken stock and leave to cool. Add onion, celery, thyme, salt and pepper and chicken stock and cook for about an hour in a fairly hot oven, gas mark 5, 375°F, 190°C.

Section Four

Main Courses *or*
Prime Minister's Question Time

Main Courses *or* Prime Minister's Question Time

Critics of the proceedings of Parliament now highlight Prime Minister's Question Time as little more than a showcase for aspiring MPs to show off with sycophantic praise for policy or bench thumping personal rebukes and jibes.

Soon after the Election the Labour Government decided that Question Time would be changed from two sessions per week to one half hour session on a Wednesday afternoon.

However, to the public either viewing at home on television or having queued for hours outside for admission to the galleries, it remains perhaps the most popular session in the Commons. For the Prime Minister it can be a soundbite triumph or an opposition glee filled disaster.

Certainly to be involved in the scrum for seats, or to prepare for countless bobbing up and down to catch the Speaker's eye, to ask a Question, MPs will need a well nourished and energy giving disposition, with a sound main course inside them.

PRIME MINISTER

Tony Blair

LABOUR-SEDGEFIELD

With both Tony and Cherie busy working people, this might be one to make and freeze ahead! Then with the children, all hands on deck at suppertime.

Meatball and Tomato Sauce

Ingredients:

500g minced beef

3 cloves garlic, chopped

2 tablespoons chopped fresh mint and parsley

salt and black pepper

1 egg

2 tablespoons olive oil

Tomato sauce:

400g can of chopped tomatoes

1 chicken or vegetable stock cube

2 tablespoons white wine

1 large onion, very finely chopped

2 tablespoons olive oil

1 fresh red or green chilli, deseeded and chopped
(omit if you don't like your food too hot)

1 tablespoon fresh parsley, basil or coriander, chopped

salt and freshly ground black pepper

Method:

Put the tomatoes and their juice in a wok with the crumbled stock cube, wine, onion, olive oil and chilli. Add the herbs, a little salt and pepper bring to simmering point, cover and let it bubble away for 5–10 minutes.

Mix together the minced meat, garlic, fresh herbs, and salt and pepper. Break the egg into it and mix it up with your hands. Form the mixture into meatballs the size of table-tennis balls. Heat the oil in a frying pan and fry the meatballs gently for 7–10 minutes. When they are cooked through, add them to the tomato sauce and serve with spaghetti, cooked al dente.

Kerry Pollard

Labour-St Albans

This recipe has a rather Hollywood sound to it but rather than tinsel town, it is hearty, substantial and with a real flavour.

Chicken Zhivago
Serves 6

Ingredients:

6 boneless chicken breasts (6-7 ozs) each

2 rounded tablespoons plain flour

1 large onion

6 rashers smoked streaky bacon

8 ozs mushrooms
2ozs butter or marg

1 pint chicken stock

3 tablespoons dry sherry or white wine

Quarter teaspoon mixed herbs

4ozs double cream

1 rounded tablespoon chopped parsley

Method:

Prepare oven gas mark 5 – 375°F or 190°C

Lay chicken flat and cut into strips half an inch thick. Toss in flour. Finely chop the onion, remove rind from the bacon and cut into strips. Slice the mushrooms. Melt 1oz butter or margarine in a frying pan, add onions and bacon and cook until tender. Add mushrooms and cook for a few more minutes. Remove from the pan, add 1oz butter and fry the chicken until brown. Stir in the stock and sherry, bring to the boil and add seasoning and herbs.

Place in a casserole cover and cook for 45 minutes. Remove from the heat and stir in the cream, cook for a further 15 minutes. Decorate with chopped parsley. Delicious served with saffron rice, green beans or green salad.

Frank Roy

Labour-Motherwell and Wishaw

Frank is another MP with a strong liking for good fresh home produced local ingredients of which he has delicately balanced with some from across the border!

Rack of Lamb

Method:

Take a suitable sized rack of Scottish lamb and crust skin with a mixture of wholemeal breadcrumbs, two level teaspoons English mustard, a few pinches of thyme, a few chopped cloves of garlic and salt and pepper.

Lamb is then cooked for about 30-40 minutes in hot oven (depending upon size).

Serve with glazed baby onions, sugar snap peas, courgettes (which have been sautéed in olive oil with chopped onion and garlic for a few minutes, seasoning and a few chopped tomatoes added at the last minute) Add rosti potatoes to complete.

Lindsay Hoyle

Labour-Chorley

Lindsay has added that good standby but once again always popular recipe that he regrets is often 'cooked for him but not by him.'

Shepherd's Pie

1 lb minced meat (lamb or beef)
1 large onion
1 carrot
1 tablespoon tomato puree
Half a pint stock
1oz cornflour
1 and a half pounds potatoes (peeled)
Salt and pepper
Cheddar Cheese

Boil potatoes, drain and mash with milk and butter. Chop the onion finely and fry until soft. Add the meat and brown. Finely grate a carrot and add to the meat. Fry for another 5 mins. Add the stock and bring to the boil. Thicken with cornflour, add tomato puree and put into a greased dish. Pipe the mashed potato over the top and sprinkle with grated cheddar cheese. Bake in oven at 180°C for about 30 minutes.

Serve with beetroot or red cabbage.

Steve McCabe

Labour-Birmingham Hall Green

A fresh and delicate combination of ingredients for another chicken recipe.

Tarragon Cream Chicken
Serves 4

Ingredients:

4 chicken breasts
Plain flour
Black pepper
Approx 60g of butter
1 chopped leek
1 cup of dry white wine, 1 cup of chicken stock
Half a teaspoons of dried tarragon leaves
Quarter of a cup of cream

Method:

Trim fillets and toss in flour seasoned with pepper. Heat butter in a frying pan. Add fillets and cook over medium heat for about 1-2 minutes, turning once. Remove chicken and lightly grill for a few minutes until cooked, but do not overcook. Add leeks to pan and cook until coloured, sprinkle through a couple of teaspoons of remaining flour. Pour wine and stock into pan and stir until mixture begins to simmer. Add tarragon and simmer uncovered for about 8-10 minutes. Return chicken to the pan and simmer uncovered for 2-3 minutes. Add cream, garnish and serve with new potatoes and green beans.

Patrick Hall

Labour–Bedford and Kempston

Born, bred and worked all his professional life in Bedford Patrick has sent in a 'light' curry meal, which again highlights the popularity of curries within our daily diet these days.

Patrick's Light Curry

Ingredients: for 4 people

8 chicken thighs

1 spanish onion – diced

garlic paste 2 green chillies – finely chopped

olive oil – 1 jar Patak's Balti paste

1 cup of white wine

2-3 tablsps of natural yoghurt
3 tomatoes – cut into eighths
fresh coriander

Method:

Marinade (preferably overnight in the fridge) chicken thighs in well stirred mix of 3 tablsps of Balti paste, 2-3 tablsps of yoghurt, the white wine and garlic paste. Remove thighs from mix carefully taking off any excess of fluid. Heat 3 tablsps of olive oil in a large frying pan, dice the onion and cook until translucent, cook in the chillies for 3-5 minutes. Seal the thighs on all sides in the pan. Remove the contents of the pan into a flat bottomed baking dish that will give a snug fit. Pour the remainder of the marinade mix between the thighs taking care to leave the skin exposed in order that it may brown when cooking. Wedge the tomatoes between the thighs and place in the oven for 1 hour 20 minutes at 180°F.

Chop the coriander and sprinkle over generously before serving. Serve with basmati rice and/or naan bread.

Kelvin Hopkins

Labour-Luton North

Kelvin has chosen this Italian influenced recipe which he says is genuinely one of his favourite quick meals. He also says that as the main cook in his house, he also enjoys eating it too!

Fusili Carbonara con funghi

Ingredients:

4 oz wholemeal fusili
3 cloves garlic
3 tablespoons olive oil
2 rashers thick smoked back bacon
3 oz field mushrooms
1 large fresh free-range egg
2 tablespoons fresh single cream
Grated parmesan and black pepper

Method:

Crush the garlic and fry in olive oil until golden brown. Remove garlic from oil and fry the chopped bacon, first removing the fat. When the bacon is well cooked, remove from oil, and fry the mushrooms, finely sliced. Simmer fusili until cooked (slightly al dente), drain water from saucepan, add lightly stirred raw egg to pasta immediately, and stir in well. Mix in fried bacon and mushrooms. Add cream and stir again. Serve immediately with grated parmesan and black pepper, accompanied by glass of Chianti Classico 1990 (or equivalent).

BUONO APPETITO

Des Turner

Labour–Brighton Kemptown

The sudden flurry of Sussex Labour MPs has brought a change of political colour right into the heart of this seaside resort – but rather than the traditional fish and chips, Des has offered his own local taste of the sea.

Scallops à la Kemptown
Serves 4

Ingredients:

1 and a half lbs (700g) fresh tomatoes – skinned and chopped coarsely
1 lb (450g) small button chestnut mushrooms
2 cloves garlic – finely chopped 1 fresh red chilli – deseeded and finely chopped
1 and a half tablsps olive oil largish sprig of fresh thyme
Zest and juice of 2 oranges
12 fresh scallops with their coral (if frozen 16)
Handful of fresh coriander – chopped salt, ground pepper and sugar to taste

Method:

Briefly fry the garlic and chilli in the olive oil and then add the chopped tomatoes and the thyme. Simmer for a few minutes until the tomatoes start to soften and then add the whole button mushrooms and the juice and zest of the oranges. Simmer for 10 minutes and then try for seasoning. If the tomatoes are not vine-ripened you may have to add a little sugar. Add the scallops.

To serve hot: Poach the scallops for 2 minutes, scatter on the coriander and serve with spiced basmati rice or couscous.

To serve cold: Poach the scallops for one minute and leave to cool. If not eating immediately refrigerate until 15 minutes before the meal. Scatter with the coriander just before serving and accompany with garlic bread.

Syd Rapson

Labour-Portsmouth North

Syd has definitely thought of a stock cupboard and greengrocers' winner here. Well worth the wait and the preparation!

Homemade Stew

Using leftovers from the Sunday roast i.e. chicken or beef, finely chopped. Add to cubed carrots, parsnips, turnips swede and leeks. Also add 5 cloves of chopped garlic. Cover in stock and simmer for approximately 2 hours. Add some oxtail stock (best to consult with Madam Speaker!) and simmer for 15 minutes. Serve with crusty French bread.

Christopher Leslie

Labour-Shipley

MPs worried about too much fat content in their sedentary lifestyle can take heart from this delicious fish recipe.

Smoked mackerel and spinach fishcakes
Serves 4

Ingredients:

2 smoked mackerel, about 150g each
2 teaspoons olive oil
125g cooked spinach
50g butter
4 potatoes, boiled and mashed
2 eggs beaten
2 tblsps finely chopped fresh dill
half a teaspoon freshly grated nutmeg
salt and pepper
150ml natural yoghurt

Methods:

Heat the grill and place the smoked mackerel underneath, drizzled with olive oil. Cook for about 3 minutes on each side. Carefully flake the skin off the fish.

Place the spinach in a saucepan with a tiny knob of butter and dry out over medium heat. Place the mackerel and spinach in a bowl with the butter, mashed potatoes, egg, dill, nutmeg, salt and pepper. Add yoghurt to mix to a fairly firm consistency; if it is too sloppy the fishcakes will not hold their shape. Take a large egg sized amount of mixture in your hands and form into a flat cake. You should make 4 large fishcakes.

Place under the grill and cook for 5-10 minutes, turning once. Serve hot.

Ruth Kelly

Labour-Bolton West

The former economics writer and employee of the Bank of England has offered this recipe which was brought back by her husband from Ferrara, a beautiful old city in the heart of north-east Italy's 'Red Belt' – that section of the Po Plain that has been showing New Labour since the last war that it is possible to combine left-of-centre popular government with a vibrant agriculture sector and a strong industrial base.

Tortelli di Zucca or Cappellaci di Zucca

Ruth says that although there is a wide variety of commercially-produced stuffed pasta – ravioli, tortellini, cappelletti – available in most supermarkets, you will not find this version and people will be surprised by its combination of the sweet flavour of pumpkin with other savoury ingredients.

Pasta: For six people make a hollow in 500g of strong flour and mix in 5 beaten eggs and 5 teaspoons of milk to make the Tortellini easier to seal. Knead the mixture until smooth adding more flour if it is too sticky and roll it out into a sheet.

Filling: Clean 1 and a half kilos of pumpkin, or 800gs of sweet potato if pumpkin is not available and bake it in the oven until tender, up to an hour. Allow to cool and after peeling the pumpkin or potato blend it with 200g of freshly grated parmesan, an egg yolk, 3 tblsp of finely chopped parsley 25 g of prosciutto ham or green bacon (leave out for vegetarians) and a generous teaspoon of nutmeg (a basic and important element of the cooking of the Emilia Romagna region).

Cut circles of pasta with a cutter or glass, place a teaspoon of the mixture on it and roll up and seal the edges. Cook in salted boiling water, drain and serve with melted butter and parmesan cheese or a little ragu.

Traditionally eaten on Christmas Eve or New Year, but delicious any time of the year!

Tony McWalter

Labour/Co-Op-Hemel Hempstead

Tony has been very honest and admitted this delicious recipe comes from Leck, the proprietor of the local restaurant and pub very near to his constituency office! The pub specialises in Thai food and Leck is Thai herself. We hope Tony has registered this (wonderful) connection in the Members' Register of Interests!

Kai Phat Med
(Stir Fried chicken with cashew nuts)
Serves 4

Ingredients:

300g sliced chicken breast

2 tablespoons vegetable oil

quarter tablespoon chopped garlic

quarter cup freshly roasted cashew nuts

quarter cup thinly sliced dried chillies

1 small onion sliced

1 third cup spring onions cut into short lengths

1 and a half tablespoon oyster sauce

1 tablespoon tomato sauce

1 red spur chilli sliced

4- 5 coriander leaves

1 red pepper and 1 green pepper cut into strips

Method:

Heat wok over medium heat. Fry garlic – when it has yellowed add chicken and cook for 3 minutes turning regularly. Add cashew nuts dried chillis, onion, spring onion, tomato sauce, oyster sauce, peppers and salt. Cook for 4 minutes. Garnish with spring onions chilli and coriander leaves. Serve with plain boiled basmati rice.

Phil Woolas

Labour-Oldham East and Saddleworth

Phil says his is not an original recipe, but one that probably goes back to the war of the Roses. However, this version is recalled from his school cook, Bertha Williams at Worsthorne County Primary School, near Lancashire. When the school house moved to its new building in 1968 there was a new kitchen and Bertha went into overdrive. 'Everyday', he says, 'we had a different home cooked meal'.

Lancashire Hot Pot
Serves 4

Ingredients:

2lbs Scrag End, i.e. best neck of mutton
3 lamb kidneys
3 large onions
2 lbs old potatoes
Butter, salt and pepper and stock

Method:

As this is a casserole, not a pie, the making is in the layering.

Slice the potatoes and lay half of them along the bottom of a greased casserole dish. Sprinkle with salt and pepper. Chop the meat into small cubes and lay across the potatoes. Slice the onions and layer them next. Pour over stock. Cover with remaining sliced potatoes. Brush the top of the potatoes with a generous amount of melted butter to make the top crisp. Cook at Gas mark 3 for 2 hours 30 minutes.

Ian Stewart

Labour-Eccles

Surprisingly we had only one savoury recipe that was doubled up on so for fairness compare and contrast this offering from Ian with that from Phil. May the best Hot Pot win! Pity we couldn't have Bertha from the school to judge!

Lancashire Hot Pot
(Version 2)
Serves 4

Ingredients:

6 or 7 large potatoes (peeled and sliced quarter of an inch thick)

3 large onions (sliced in rings)

4 carrots (sliced)

4 lamb chops

spoon of chopped fresh parsley

2-3 sprigs fresh rosemary

half a pint meat stock

1 finely chopped garlic clove

cup of water

salt and freshly ground black pepper

vegetable oil or butter

Method:

Cover the bottom of a large deep oven – proof dish with a layer of onion, then add a layer of potato and carrot. Repeat until the dish is half full, seasoning with the salt and pepper, rosemary and parsley. Add the lamb chops, smeared with the chopped garlic, then continue the layering until the dish is full. The top layer should be entirely potato, which should be brushed with the butter or the vegetable oil. Place in a preheated oven, covered with foil, at about 200°C and cook for about one and a half hours. Remove foil and cook further (about another hour) or until the potatoes have gone brown and crunchy on top. Serve with pickled vegetables, such as cabbage, onion or beetroot.

LET BATTLE COMMENCE!

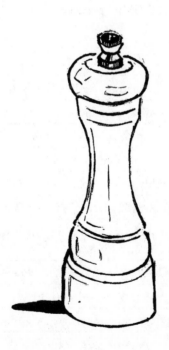

Shona McIsaac

Labour-Cleethorpes

Shona who is the daughter of a cook found it a daunting prospect to come up with a favourite recipe. But in the end she has chosen two fish dishes – both her own creations. Shona puts down food writer as her profession and has written freelance for many magazines – we feel she knows her subject pretty well!

Smoked haddock, cauliflower and potato bake

Based on cauliflower cheese making a warming and filling winter meal
Serves 4

Ingredients:

7oz baby new potatoes, washed but skins left on

8oz cauliflower, divided into florets

9oz smoked haddock fillet

Semi skimmed milk

Freshly ground black pepper

4oz peeled cooked prawns (thawed if frozen)

Cheese sauce (make your own using the reserved milk or for speed use ready made)

2oz smoked cheddar (or other hard cheese) grated

Pinch of grated nutmeg

Pinch of cayenne or piri-piri seasoning

Fresh chopped parsley to garnish

Method:

Boil new potatoes and cauliflower in separate pans until just done. Drain and set aside. Place haddock in a frying pan and cover with milk. Season with black pepper. Bring to the boil, turn off the heat, cover and leave for five minutes. Drain off the milk and reserve for cheese sauce. Arrange potatoes and cauliflower in a gratin dish. Flake the fish and scatter over the potatoes and cauliflower with the prawns. Make the cheese sauce. Season the sauce with cayenne or piri-piri, grated nutmeg and freshly ground black pepper. Sprinkle the grated cheese over and place in oven until cheese bubbles. Garnish with parsley to serve.

Ceviche Salad
(adapted from a South American recipe)
Serves 4

A great summer salad. The lime juice 'cooks' the fish, turning it white, while giving it a tangy and spicy flavour. It's high in fibre and low in fat – a really healthy meal.

Ingredients:

4 thin skinless fresh haddock fillets
2 limes, thinly sliced
1 red pepper, deseeded and sliced
1 yellow pepper
1 red onion, peeled and sliced
Fresh coriander leaves
Juice of 4 limes/2 lemons
1 tablespoon extra virgin olive oil
1 fresh red chilli, deseeded and sliced
1 teaspoon soft brown sugar
Baby spinach leaves
Watercress

Method:

Cut the haddock into thin strips and then 2.5 cm lengths. Wipe the base of a glass dish with a slice of lime. Arrange fish in the dish, alternating with the peppers, limes, onions and coriander. Mix together the lime juice, lemon juice, oil chopped chilli and sugar. Pour over the salad ensuring the fish is well covered. Cover the dish and leave to marinate in the fridge for four hours. Prepare the salad leaves and arrange in a large glass salad bowl. Lift out the ceviche ingredients with a slotted spoon and heap onto the salad leaves. Serve with crusty bread.

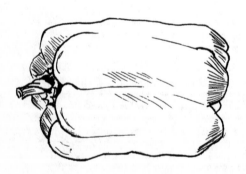

Andrew Dismore

Labour-Hendon

Andrew claims this is not a 'favourite' but more practical for those at Westminster who retreat to their London attics for a break – one for Members who are not able to get to the shops on a regular basis and just keep a few tins on the shelf

Spaghetti Puttanesca

Ingredients:

1 can of anchovies (snip the anchovies)

1 can of plum peeled tomatoes (Italian)

1 bottle of Passata (Italian sieved tomatoes)

Chillies (amount according to taste)

Small can of pitted black olives (chopped)

Garlic (crushed) amount according to taste

Basil leaves, Olive Oil and Spaghetti

Method:

Begin by heating the olive oil in a solid pan and gently saute the garlic and chilli(es), taking care not to burn the garlic. Then add the anchovies and stir round. Add the chopped olives and torn basil leaves (stir) followed by the passata and tinned tomatoes. Bring to the boil and then simmer on a very low heat until you are left with a thick sauce. In the meantime boil the spaghetti according to taste. When the spaghetti is cooked, strain and add a small amount of the sauce to the strained pasta and stir to ensure that all strands are coated. Before serving the sauce add a few more torn basil leaves.

You can use Parmesan with this dish. However, Italian gastronomists shudder at the thought of Parmesan being added to sauces containing fish! *Bon Appetito!*

Paul Keetch

Liberal Democrat-Hereford

Paul keeps to the Italian theme for his recipe, another variation for lovers of spaghetti.

Spaghetti alla Carbonara
Serves 2

Ingredients:

Spaghetti (allow 4-5 oz per person)

8 oz smoked streaky bacon or pancetta

1-2 cloves garlic

1 oz butter

3 eggs

2-3 fl ozs single cream

4 oz button mushrooms(optional)

Sea salt and freshly milled black pepper

Methods:

Gently melt the butter and fry the bacon or pancetta until crispy. Add crushed garlic and mushrooms if using. Whilst the bacon is cooking, beat the eggs lightly together with the cream and salt and pepper to taste. Meanwhile boil a large pan of water ready for the spaghetti. When the water is at a rolling boil, add the spaghetti and cook according to instructions, until al dente. Quickly drain the spaghetti and return to the saucepan with the bacon (and mushrooms). Off the heat add the egg and cream mixture and stir. The heat of the spaghetti will gently cook the eggs and cream. Serve with shavings of fresh parmesan, crisp breadsticks and a good chianti!

Jim Fitzpatrick

Labour–Poplar and Canning Town

As a former member of the London Fire Brigade, Jim feels there are some similarities between firefighter and MP – strange hours, bells, the requirement to be in the lobby within 8 minutes, (too) few women, predominantly male, many traditions, poles – sliding in the Fire Service or greasy (!) ones at Westminster – and lots of POSING! The main difference is that firemen are much more respected than politicians...

But even if you were rushing Jim's recipe is still quick enough to keep any home fire burning!

Pasta with Pesto Sauce and Garlic Bread

Ingredients:

Fresh pasta (buy a packet to suit numbers to feed)

Jar(s) or pesto – red or green

Dash of single cream

French stick – sliced

Butter/margarine and cloves of fresh garlic crushed and mixed

Method

Boil fresh pasta (minutes) drain, add pesto (cream already mixed) and stir.

Easy – 10 minutes for a Main Meal – Don't forget the wine (red or white!)

Dr Ian Gibson

Labour-Norwich North

A scientist by profession Ian has not got too technical with his dish – the method here still remains easy to follow!

Southern Fried Chicken

Ingredients:

2.5 lbs (1.1 kg) chicken pieces
2 oz (50 g) plain flour
1 tablespoon (15 ml) spoon salt
4 oz (100g) butter
8 tablespoons (8 x 15ml) sunflower oil
Cream Gravy
1 tablespoon (15ml spoon) arrowroot or cornflour
Quarter pint chicken stock
Quarter pint single cream
Salt and freshly ground black pepper

Method:

Dry the chicken pieces with kitchen towel. Mix the flour and salt, put in a strong bag and shake a few pieces of chicken in the bag to coat evenly with the seasoned flour. Continue until all chicken pieces are covered. Heat the butter and oil in a large frying pan that can easily hold all the chicken pieces or use a smaller pan and do half at a time. When the fat is very hot and beginning to bubble, add chicken pieces, skin side down, starting with the thighs and legs to allow a longer cooking time. When brown on one side then turn and brown the other side. Reduce the heat cover the pan and continue cooking until the pieces are done – 15 minutes.

Remove the chicken from the pan and keep it warm in a low oven. Gravy – Pour off all but 2 tablespoons of the fat from the pan (this can be strained and used again) Stir in the arrowroot or cornflour and then the stock and cream. Cook for a few minutes, stirring with whisk until the gravy is thick. Season with salt and pepper and serve in a gravy boat to pour over the chicken.

Anne Begg

Labour–Aberdeen South

Anne, an English teacher by profession, has given a home cooked pair of warming recipes to cast away the coldest of Scottish winds.

My Mother's Meat Roll

Ingredients:

1lb minced meat
Quarter pound bacon, minced
Small onion, chopped
2 cups breadcrumbs
1 tblsp dry bisto
1 oxo cube dissolved in three quarters cup boiling water
1 tblsp tomato sauce

Method:

Mix all ingredients together. Put mixture into a greased steaming bowl or meat roll jar. Cover with greaseproof paper then tin foil and tie tightly with string. Steam for 2 hours. Pour off excess gravy which can be used to make stovies (see below). If mince was made from lean beef then there may be very little gravy. Turn out meat roll onto a plate and allow to cool. Wrap in tin foil and chill in fridge prior to slicing.

Stovies (stoved potatoes)

Ingredients:

Gravy (from meat roll or roast beef or left over stew
or mushroom ketchup)

Chopped onions

Sliced potatoes

Bisto gravy powder

Method:

Soften onion and potatoes in gravy. Add water if too dry. Add
bisto dissolved in cold water. Simmer for half to three quarters of
an hour until potatoes are all mushy.

Dr George Turner

A very oriental recipe here which George says has evolved over a number of years to its present form after the original recipe was obtained from some long forgotten book.

Turner's Thai Treat

Ingredients:

---

4 boneless skinless chicken breasts

---

1 tablespoon sesame oil
3 small chopped fresh red chillies
2 cups coconut milk

---

2 tablespoons fish sauce
2 tablespoons lime juice half a cup peanuts,
finely chopped

---

2 tblsp chopped fresh coriander

(Adjust quantity of chillies according to strength
and your own taste!)

Curry paste

---

3 chopped dried chillies

---

1 dried kaffir lime leaf

Half a teaspoon galangal powder

---

1 chopped stem fresh lemon grass
1 teaspoon shrimp powder
2 small chopped onions

Half a teaspoon ground coriander

---

1 tblsp fish sauce

---

2 tblsp crunchy peanut butter

(Curry paste will keep, covered, in a fridge for 2 weeks)

Method:

Curry paste: Blend together the lime leaf, galangal, lemon grass, shrimp powder, chillies and boiling water and leave to infuse for 20 minutes. Drain and discard liquid. Mix together with remaining ingredients to form a coarse paste.

Thai Treat: Cut each breast into three and slice thinly. Heat the oil in a large pan and stir fry the chicken slices until well browned. Remove from the pan. Combine 2 tablespoons of curry paste with the chillies in the pan. Stir over heat for about 2 minutes or until fragrant. Add coconut milk, fish sauce, lime juice and peanuts and bring to the boil, stirring continuously. Add the cooked chicken to the pan and simmer, covered, for about 5 minutes or until the chicken is tender. Just before serving stir in the coriander.

Cooked dish can be frozen successfully. Defrost and reheat thoroughly.

David Taylor

Labour/Co-Op-North West Leicestershire

A very popular dish, but with a twist of flavour that David claims is a definite winner.

Chilli Con Carne North West
Serves 4

Ingredients:

1lb mince (any sort you like)
1 tin red kidney beans
Garlic puree
1 glass red wine (at least!)
1 onion
1 tin chopped tomatoes
Tomato puree Stock cube
2 cups long grain rice
Quarter teaspoon tumeric

Method:

Dry fry the mince (in a wok if you have one) while you chop the onions. Add the onions and stir until browned. Put rice on to cook according to instructions, with tumeric in the water. Strain kidney beans, wash and leave to drain.

Add tomatoes to meat mixture. Add generous squirt of tomato and garlic pastes (to taste) Crumble stock cube and stir well. Add beans and wine and slightly increase heat. When rice is fluffy (and it will be if you don't keep lifting the lid!) drain and serve under generous amount of chilli. Is especially splendid with garlic bread on the side.

Adrian Sanders

Liberal Democrat-Torbay

With not a fish in sight – perhaps a surprise considering the coastal constituency of Adrian – this very fruity dish was passed to his wife by her mother who, as far as she can remember, got it from the Yorkshire Post!

Medallions of Pork in Orange Sauce
Serves 4

Ingredients:

4 x pork escalopes or chops from the fillet end of the leg

Half oz butter

1 tablespoon oil

1 small onion finely chopped

Grated rind and juice of an orange

2-3 tablespoons lemon juice

3 tablespoons Seville orange marmalade

Small piece of fresh ginger, peeled and finely chopped

3 inch piece of cinnamon stick

Quarter pint dry white wine

Plain flour seasoned with salt and pepper

Method:

Toss meat in seasoned flour. Heat oil and butter in large saucepan and quickly seal the meat. Remove from pan. Sauté onions until soft and golden in same pan (add more oil/butter if needed but keep to a minimum) Add all other ingredients to pan (except the meat) and stir well. Return meat to pan and simmer gently for 45 minutes.

Philip Hammond

Conservative-Runnymede and Weybridge

Philip attended University College Oxford, so perhaps many a night revising for his MA in Politics Philosophy and Economics was spent stocking up on this recipe.

University Pie

Ingredients:

1lb minced lamb or beef
2 medium sized onions
1 large carrot, chopped
1 cup frozen peas
1 level tablespoon flour
Half teaspoon mixed herbs
Half teaspoon chilli powder
Half pint of hot beef or lamb stock
1 tablespoon tomato puree salt and pepper
For the topping: 2lbs potatoes 2oz butter 2oz cheese Salt and pepper

Method:

Pre heat the oven to 200°C. Fry the onion until soft, then add the carrot and minced meat and cook for 5 minutes until the mixture has browned a little. Season with the salt and pepper and add herbs and spices to taste. Stir in flour mix. mixed with the herbs and chilli powder, and the tomato puree with the hot stock and add to the meat mixture. Bring to simmering point and add the frozen peas. Simmer for approx 40 minutes. If using cooked meat reduce this to 10 minutes.

Topping: Meanwhile boil the potatoes in salted water. When they are soft, cream together with butter and milk. Add half the grated cheese and season to taste. Put the meat mixture into a well greased baking dish. Spread the potato mixture on the top. Sprinkle the remaining cheese over it and bake for about 20 minutes.

Laurence Robertson

Conservative-Tewkesbury

Supplying us with a very popular, and now almost 'traditional' dish that often graces many a dinner party setting, Laurence has slightly jazzed up even this rich recipe.

Duck a l'orange

Ingredients:

4lb (1.8kg) Duck, dressed weight
Salt and black pepper
10oz (25g) butter
5 fl oz (150ml) Cointreau
1tablespoon (15ml) wine vinegar
Juice of 1 orange
5 fl oz (150ml) beef stock
2 teaspoons (10ml) cornflour
4 medium-sized oranges, peeled and cut into segments Watercress

Method:

Rinse and thoroughly dry the duck. Sprinkle salt and pepper inside the cavity. Prick skin all over with a skewer or fork. Melt the butter in a flameproof casserole or large frying pan, just large enough to contain the duck, and sauté the duck until golden on all sides. Reduce the heat and continue to sauté gently, covered, for about thirty minutes, turning the duck from time to time. Add two thirds of the cointreau and allow to simmer for a few minutes more. Remove the duck from the pan and skim the fat from the juices. Return the duck to the pan. Add the wine vinegar, orange juice and beef stock and bring to the boil. Cover, lower heat and simmer gently for about 20 minutes. Just before serving, remove the duck and keep it hot on a warm serving dish in a low oven. Place the pan/casserole on a high heat and bring the liquid to the boil, stirring constantly and scraping the sides of the casserole dish. Reduce the heat and simmer for a further ten minutes. Skim off the fat and pass the sauce through a fine sieve. Season generously with salt and pepper and add the remaining cointreau. In a small pan blend the cornflour with some of the cointreau flavoured sauce until smooth. Pour on the remaining sauce and place the pan over a moderate heat. Bring to the boil and whisk the sauce constantly, then lower the heat and simmer the sauce for a further 4-5 minutes, until slightly thickened. Add half the orange segments and simmer a little longer to heat through. To serve, pour a little sauce around the duck and garnish with fresh orange segments and watercress. Serve the sauce separately.

Derek Wyatt

Labour-Sittingbourne and Sheppey

The flamboyant Derek, whose past jobs have included being director of the computer channel at BSkyB, recalls past travels abroad with a recipe from "Le Patron of Auberge 'd'chez eux'" which Derek claims is 'simply the best restaurant in Paris'

Saddle of Rabbit with mustard
Preparation time: 40 minutes, Cooking time: 40 minutes
Serves 4

Ingredients:

A saddle of rabbit of approx half a pound (generous) per person

Mustard-type 'moutarde de Meaux'

Salt and pepper

1 cup (generous) of fresh cream.

Concentrated veal juice

Method:

Brush the inside of the saddles generously with the mustard and close the flanks to keep the mustard inside during cooking. Preheat the oven (400°F for 15 minutes) Put the saddles, flanks on top in a baking dish and cook each side for 10 minutes. Take the dish out of the oven and keep the saddles warm until you have made the sauce. Put the fresh cream in the dish and reduce it over a high heat. Add salt and pepper and finally a big spoon of mustard. Then carve the saddles without forgetting fillets and kidneys. Cover them with hot sauce and serve.

Helen Brinton

Labour-Peterborough

Helen, already marked down as one of 'Blair's leading babes' has come out with a firm strong favourite here that because of its meat content, cuts through any pretence of the 'nanny state' syndrome. Her spelling, however, is slightly mystifying!

Beouf Borgiyone

Ingredients:

2 lb stewing steak
10oz streaky bacon
8oz carrots
Half a pound mushrooms
Half a bottle of cheap red wine
Half a pint of good stock (may need topping up in the cooking)
2 onions 14 shallots Salt and pepper Mixed herbs
Tablespoon of white flour 2oz butter/margarine

Methods:

Chop stewing steak into bite sized portions then coat with mix of flour, seasoning and herbs. Fry until basted Chop bacon into bite sized pieces. Add to the pan plus shallots and onion. Add the steak and wine. Check for seasoning. Add carrots (chopped) Bring to the boil with the stock, then simmer on a very low heat for two and a half to three hours. Half an hour before serving add chopped mushrooms. 'This dish is best served with French or garlic bread, a mixed salad and new potatoes. A good bottle of Beaujolais or Pinot Noir goes well too!'

Christine Butler

Labour-Castlepoint

Christine has put down as one of her former professions 'sculptor' so we notice a slight artistic quality to this tasty dish.

Spicy Chicken in Filo Pastry Parcels

Ingredients:

Filo pastry
Chicken breast(s)
1 and a half oz peeled prawns
1 tablespoon greek yoghurt
1 tablespoon creme fraiche
Half teaspoon grated fresh ginger
1 oxo stock cube (Indian flavour)
3 small mushrooms chopped into small pieces
A dash of Thai fish sauce
A dash of tabasco sauce
2 tablespoons finely chopped fresh mint
Geeta's pineapple chutney

Methods:

Cut the chicken breast(s) into very thin strips. Cut the prawns into small pieces. Mix together in a basin the yoghurt, creme fraiche, ground black pepper, Thai fish sauce, and tabasco sauce. Into this mixture crumble the stock cube and finely chopped mint. Add the chicken, prawns and mushrooms to the cream mixture and set aside. Take 3 squares of filo pastry, butter the first sheet on both sides, adding the second sheet and butter and then the third sheet, also buttered.

If making small parcels suitable for a dinner party put a small spoonful in the middle of the sheets and a larger amount if making parcels suitable for a main course. Pull all corners up and twist slightly to seal. Place on an oiled baking sheet and bake at Gas Mark 6 220°C/400°F until golden brown. Serve immediately.

Serve with Geeta's Pineapple chutney, rice, or small sauté potatoes and a mixed salad.

Malcolm Savidge

Labour-Aberdeen North

Malcolm says he finds little time for catering now. His recipe was a dish he cooked on several occasions when entertaining a few years ago. He gleaned the Pork Chop recipe from Audrey Ellis' "Step by Step Guide to Meat Cookery" book and the accompanying saffron rice from "500 Recipes: Bedsitter cookery" by Marguerite Patten, whose directions are marvellous (just right for someone new to cooking who lives in a bedsitter!)

Pork Chops with orange honey glaze

Ingredients:

4 pork chops
1 tablespoon corn oil
2 teaspoons soya sauce
2 tablespoons honey
1 chicken stock cube
1 tablespoon tomato puree
1 orange

Method:

Fry the pork chops gently on both sides in the oil until lightly browned. Add the soy sauce, honey and stock cube and tomato puree dissolved in half a pint of boiling water. Finely pare the zest of orange and squeeze juice, and add both to the sauce. Cover pan, reduce heat and continue cooking for 20 minutes. Cook the saffron rice (see below) and spread on warmed serving dish, arrange the chops on top and continue cooking the sauce until it has reduced to the consistency of a glaze. Pour glaze over the chops, garnish with parsley sprigs.

Saffron Rice

Ingredients:

1 small cup Patna rice
2 cups cold water (use the same cup)
Half teaspoon salt
Pinch powdered saffron
Half – 1oz butter
1–2oz walnuts or almonds

Method:

Wash the rice, unless using pre-packed, ready washed rice. If washing the rice in cold water USE at once to prevent it becoming sticky. Tip the rice and water into a large saucepan (one with a tight fitting lid) add the salt and saffron and bring to the boil, stir once with a fork. Lower the heat, replace the lid and simmer for about 15 minutes without stirring or removing the lid. Test the rice by biting a few grains, if not quite tender, or if the liquid is not quite absorbed replace the lid and cook for a few minutes longer. When dry and fluffy remove from the heat. Fork in the butter and chopped nuts and serve.

Peter Bradley

Labour–The Wrekin

Peter claims no pre-eminence or, for that matter, imagination in cooking. However, this is always a favourite and worth repeating.

Spaghetti Bolognaise

Cover the bottom of a heavy pan with olive oil. Chop two onions and fry in the pan until lightly browned. Add chopped green, red and yellow peppers and crushed garlic. Stir and fry gently. Then add four large chopped mushrooms and continue to fry for 5 minutes. Then add 1lb of best lean mince and cook until fat is absorbed. Add quarter pint beef stock and simmer until liquid is absorbed. Add salt and pepper, mixed herbs and a jar of Passata. Simmer until liquid is absorbed then add quarter bottle of red wine and finally, when liquid is absorbed add and stir in a tin of chopped tomatoes. When the spaghetti is cooked, arrange on a plate, smear with butter and sprinkle with black pepper before serving the bolognaise. For best results cook the bolognaise for 90 minutes, stirring frequently.

Eat, drink and be merry!

Bob Laxton

Labour-Derby North

Bob has sent us some interesting ingredients for this unusual fish curry but left us with no guidance on method! We assume like most curries begin with frying plenty of onions and perhaps garlic and then add the following ingredients – but no doubt many readers will have their own favourite tried and tested curry night alternatives that can be adapted!

Fijian Fish Curry

Bob's Ingredients:

Pilchards
Cauliflower
Butter
Curry powder
Pinch of chilli.

Serve with plenty of rice and usual tasty accompaniments.

John Grogan

Labour-Selby

John's Constituency Office Manager, Margaret Hall has had the grace to divulge her Yorkshire Pudding recipe to him. Yorkshire Puddings are delicious with any roast, though traditionally in Yorkshire they are served as a starter just with gravy from the roast. You can, of course serve them with the roast – perhaps instead of potatoes – or with them if you're feeling really hungry! Yorkshire Puddings may also be served as a hot dessert with caramel or lemon sauce etc (leave out the pepper!) but that may be frowned upon by true Yorkshire Pudding Aficionados!

Grease 12 small bun tins (a well used tin is best). Add just under half a teaspoon of lard or fat from the roast beef (yes, lard or dripping!) to each tin and place near the top of a hot oven – gas 7, elec 425°F or 220°C. For gas use roasting oven and place on top shelf. Leave tin in oven for about 5-10 minutes whilst you prepare the mixture.

To mix the ingredients you will need a large bowl with a hand-whisk or a food processor does the job even better – you need to get lots of air into this mixture.

Ingredients:

4 oz plain flour

Pinch of salt and some freshly ground pepper

7 fl oz milk topped up to 10 fl oz with water

One large egg

Method:

Mix together, adding a good drop of liquid each time into bowl – add one large egg which you have already beaten – mix well until bubbles rise on the top of the mixture – allow to stand for a few minutes.

Take Yorkshire Pudding tins out of the oven – they should be sizzling now and when you hold the tins up you should see smoke! Immediately pour in the Yorkshire pudding mixture two-thirds up each tin – should easily fill 10-12 of the tins – do this quickly or you'll lose heat from the tins – you could use top of oven to help retain some heat whilst you do this. Put tin straight back into the oven and leave for about 15 minutes. Cook at a hot temperature on a high shelf as above leaving enough space for the puddings to rise! (Aga – use 2nd shelf to cook the puddings)

Gwyn Prosser

Labour-Dover and Deal

Gwyn has spent a lifetime afloat in one shape or form but has now laid anchor in Dover. He says 'White Cliffs Country in my beautiful constituency of Dover and Deal will be the first corner of these islands to greet the first dawn of the new millennium. The millennium sunrise will break across South Foreland which is situated above our famous White Cliffs between Dover and Deal at 07.58 on January 1st, 2000 and if you can't join us in Dover on that special morning why not celebrate the day by enjoying this recipe'. We can already see Peter Mandelson marketing it for the Dome restaurant!

Dover Sole à la Millennium Sunrise

Allow one whole Dover Sole per person – for best results use freshly landed fish caught on the Dover side of the English Channel!

Skin sole on both sides and place in grill pan which has been brushe with melted maitre d'hotel butter, then liberally apply more melted butter to the sole. Sprinkle with salt and freshly ground pepper and place under a pre-heated medium grill for 5 minutes. Turn over the sole, rebutter the fish and grill for a further 5 minutes or so. Serve immediately from the sizzling grill pan, surround each fish with lemon slices, garnish with parsley and add one generous butter pat to each Dover Sole to give an attractive 'millennium sunrise effect'.

Section Five

Vegetarian dishes *or* the Division Bell

Vegetarian dishes *or* the Division Bell

New MPs are often astonished by the small size of the House of Commons when they first enter it. At the Opening of Parliament and in important debates, MPs are struggling for seats being careful not to overstep the sword line that keeps them from 'crossing the floor' to an opposing political party. It is very cramped and at no time is this more apparent than when a crucial vote takes place in the lobby corridors. A division is another word for a vote. Within the House the question is put on a matter within a debate and 'aye' (or yes) or 'no' are then called in the chamber itself. The Speaker will then say 'I think the ayes have it' or 'I think the noes have it'. If the result seems close and is challenged by MPs then an order is given to 'clear the lobby' and the division bell sounds.

On either side of the Chamber of the House of Commons, tellers' doors are locked and division bells continue sounding throughout all the parliamentary buildings. Those voting 'aye' go to the right side and 'no' to the left. There is a time limit of eight minutes to register one's vote, and often MPs are seen running from outside buildings into the chamber, or responding to pagers to record their vote. Strangely MPs can vote in a division even though they were not present to hear the original question – needless to say they probably would have had prior knowledge that the subject was being raised. No MP is obliged to vote. However, Governments with tiny majorities (and even today's with its large majority), like to keep their MPs in line supporting the party Whips working in adjacent offices are often out with reminders or sterner techniques to ensure that all votes are placed, except in exceptional circumstances. During such a division an MP can raise a point of order, but he/she must remain seated and must wear a hat. A collapsible top hat is kept within the chamber for just such a purpose – and was recently used in the controversial fox hunting debate.

With a vast array of recipes in this section we think on the question of favouring vegetables 'The Ayes have it.'

Michael Foster

Labour-Worcester

There being two Michael Fosters' in Parliament, should not have caused that much difficulty, but when this Michael Foster drew first choice in the ballot for Private Member's Bills in the first session of Parliament, and then promptly chose a controversial proposal to ban fox hunting, it was inevitable that his name would become famous, or perhaps to some sections infamous. Whilst the debate goes on, Michael has non-controversially sent us his favourite vegetarian dish.

Courgettes and Tomato Au Gratin

Ingredients:

4 medium courgettes, sliced (but not peeled)

2 tblsps olive oil

1 large clove garlic, crushed

4oz (110g) Italian Mozzarella (or Cheddar)cheese sliced

4 large tomatoes, peeled and sliced

4 level tblsps grated Parmesan cheese

1 tblsp chopped fresh basil or 1 teaspoon dried oregano

Salt and freshly milled black pepper

Method:

Pre heat the oven to gas mark 5, 375°F (190°C)

If you have the time, salt, drain and dry the sliced courgettes. Heat the oil in a frying pan large enough to hold the courgettes in one layer (otherwise do them in two batches), add the crushed garlic and saute the courgette slices to a nice golden colour on each side. Next arrange layers of courgettes, cheese slices and sliced tomatoes in a heatproof gratin dish so that they overlap each other slightly like slates on a roof. Finally sprinkle on the grated Parmesan, basil or oregano and salt and freshly milled pepper. Then bake on a high shelf in the oven for 30 minutes. Serve this with lots of crusty bread and a green salad with a sharp lemony dressing.

Jane Griffiths

Labour–Reading East

Jane has travelled extensively with her previous work as Foreign News Editor with the BBC World Service so this recipe has a typical Mediterranean feel.

Ratatouille Charlotte

Serves 4

Ingredients:

2 herb focaccia
400g tin plum tomatoes
2 medium sized onions, chopped
2 cloves garlic, crushed
1 red pepper, finely sliced
1 tablespoon balsamic vinegar
2 tablespoon olive oil
50g goat's cheese
150ml single cream
25g butter fresh basil, finely chopped
Oregano, seasoning fresh basil leaves and shaved parmesan to garnish

Method:

Preheat oven to 200°C. Heat 1 tablespoon of oil in a large pan and fry the onions and garlic until the onions begin to brown. Add the oregano and tomatoes, breaking them down with a spoon. Cover and cook gently for 20 minutes or until the mixture begins to thicken, stirring occasionally. Leave to cool. Stir in the vinegar and season.

Butter four ramekins. Cut four circles of focaccia to fit in the base of the ramekins. Cut four further circles to place on the top of the ramekins. Cut the remaining bread into strips and line the sides of the ramekins, ensuring that the strips overlap.

Spoon approx quarter of the ratatouille into each ramekin. Top with a piece of goat's cheese and then add the remaining ratatouille. Cover with the larger bread disks, pressing down firmly. Stand the ramekins in an ovenproof dish and add boiling water to come halfway up the sides. Bake for twenty to twenty five minutes until golden.

Meanwhile heat the remaining oil in a small pan. Gently fry the peppers until soft. Allow to cool and then add the cream and fresh basil. Warm gently, but do not allow to boil.

Loosen the edges of the charlotte with a knife and turn out onto individual plates. Drizzle the sauce over the top and serve with a garnish of fresh basil and shavings of parmesan cheese.

Gillian Merron

Labour-Lincoln

Gillian has taken a recipe from Sarah Brown's Vegetarian Kitchen cookbook and tells us about the power of the dragon in the title! Aduki beans are called 'red dragon' or 'red wonder' beans by the Chinese, as they have found them to be so full of goodness. She says they are just the thing for the Labour campaigner!

Red Dragon Pie
Serves 4

Ingredients:

4 ozs /110g aduki beans
2 oz/50g rice
2 pints/1.1 litres water for soaking
2 pints/1.1 litres water for boiling
1 tablespoon oil
1 onion, peeled and finely chopped
8 oz/225g carrots, scrubbed and diced
1-2 tablespoons soy sauce
2 tablespoons tomato puree
1 teaspoon mixed herbs salt and pepper
Half pint/275 ml aduki bean stock
1lb/450g potatoes, peeled, boiled then mashed

Method:

Oven: Gas Mark 4 350°F 180°C

Wash aduki beans and rice and soak together overnight or in boiling water for 1 hour. Drain and rinse. Boil in fresh water and cook for 50 minutes or until fairly soft. Drain and keep the stock.

Heat oil and fry onion for 5 minutes. Add the carrots and cook for 2-3 minutes. Add cooked beans and rice mixture. Mix soy sauce, tomato puree and herbs with stock. Pour this over the bean and vegetable mixture. Bring to the boil, simmer for 20-30 minutes. Season to taste add a little more liquid if necessary so that final mixture is moist.

Transfer to 3 pint/1.5 litre casserole dish and cover with mashed potatoes. Bake for 35-40 minutes until potato is crisp and brown. Serve with green vegetables and a tomato sauce (ketchup will do!)

Enjoy!

Nick Palmer

Labour–Broxtowe

Nick, joint compiler of this book, is a true European, who previously both lived and worked in Switzerland and has therefore chosen this famous Swiss dish. It is similar to American hash browns but with more variations. He claims that busy people can get pre-prepared Roesti potatoes at large Marks and Spencer branches, but that these are flavoured unusually with herbs, but are otherwise convincing. But let us try the 'real thing'.

Berner Roesti
(pronounced Rooshti)

Ingredients:

2-3 spoons of cooking oil or equivalent butter

800 grams of peeled potatoes

1 coffee spoon salt

Method:

Slice the potatoes into strips (Nick says if you ever take a holiday in Switzerland you can buy a 'Roestiraffel' to help, it works like a cheese-parer).

Heat up the oil/butter. Distribute the potato strips on the pan, salt, stir, add any desired additional elements, cover, and bake until brown, shaking the pan from time to time.

Baking time 20-30 minutes.

A faster result can be achieved by frying for 8-10 minutes on a medium heat, turning after 5 minutes.

William Thompson

Ulster Unionist–Tyrone West

William has chosen a very traditional and substantial Irish dish which is simple yet delicious. It is often an addition to the main course but is just as good on its own.

Culcannon

Ingredients:

Potatoes
Leeks
Onions
Butter

Method:

Peel and chop the leeks, onions. Peel potatoes and cut into pieces. Boil all together then mash, add butter and serve.

David Prior

Conservative–Norfolk North

David has replied that we unwisely asked him for a recipe and claims not to be a cook! However, he recommend this dish and says the recipe is virtually idiot-proof so long as you don't forget and leave it in the oven for too long!

Layered Vegetables

Chop small courgettes into thin slices and place on bottom of casserole dish.

Do the same with tomatoes – you need a good layer of both.

Grate Cheddar cheese on top.

Repeat this process 3 times.

Put plenty of butter in it as well.

Finally bake in oven for half an hour so that cheese on top is well browned.

Candy Atherton

Labour-Falmouth and Camborne

It is great that Candy has thought of something simple yet spectacular, with one of the most underused vegetables we have in this country.

Posh Cabbage

Ingredients:

2lb (approx) of crisp, white cabbage
8oz salted, roasted peanuts
salt to taste

Method:

Cook cabbage in usual way until tender but still firm. Drain well and toss in peanuts. Add salt to taste and serve.

Julian Lewis

Conservative–New Forest East

Rather than a full recipe Julian has kindly laid bare one of the inner secrets of his past reckless youth! He says 'If I could recover all the money spent on eating out because of my inability to cook, I could probably afford to retire tomorrow. Yet, I do recall, as a student in the 1970s, having to fend for myself to escape the ghastly college food.

At that time (and possibly still today) it was possible to buy frozen packets of 'stir-fry' vegetables. I realised that these were prepared in a frying pan in a way very similar to the scrambling of eggs – one of the few culinary accomplishments to my credit. I therefore combined the two processes and found that the result was both psychedelic and sustaining.

I never got round to patenting this recipe and am happy to make a free gift of it to the students of the 1990s who, I am sorry to say, seem at least as impoverished as those of the 1970s.'

Jacqui Smith

Labour-Redditch

Jacqui's recipe is, she says, heavily influenced by Delia Smith. It reminds her of hot, dry days in summer when she likes to eat this dish with a glass or two of dry white wine, some fresh bread and good company.

Roasted Red Pepper with an Italian filling
Serves 4

Ingredients:

4 red peppers

16 cherry tomatoes (tinned tomatoes are OK)

8-12 anchovy fillets

1-2 cloves garlic (crushed)

a few leaves of basil (chopped) or 1 level teaspoon of mixed or Italian dried herbs are OK)

4 tablespoons of extra virgin olive oil

Method:

Halve the peppers cutting from stem to base, remove the seeds. Place the tomatoes in a bowl of boiling water for 1 minute and then remove the skins. A tin of chopped tomatoes can speed preparation time up considerably. Arrange the peppers in a heavy, shallow roasting tin so that their bodies can be filled with the other ingredients listed above apart from the oil. End the preparation with a spoonful of olive oil over each pepper. Season only with pepper to taste and roast in the top of the oven at gas mark 5 for 40 minutes.

Serve with fresh bread and the juices from the roasting tray.

Tom Brake

Liberal Democrat–Carshalton and Wallington

As a child Tom lived and was educated in France. He remembers that one of his domestic duties there was to prepare the salad for dinner. Typically this was a mixture of lettuce, tomatoes, endives or 'carottes râpées'. But whatever the salad, it required a French salad dressing. This is Tom's.

French Dressing

Ingredients:

French mustard
wine vinegar
salt and pepper
olive oil

Method:

Using a mug, teaspoon and fork. Start with a generous helping of French mustard, about half an inch in the bottom of a mug. Add vinegar (about a quarter of the volume of the mustard) and mix into a paste with the fork. Add salt and pepper to taste. Tom uses lots of the latter, hardly any of the former.

Finally pour in the olive oil. Pour it in gradually so that it remains homogenous, mixing all the time with the fork. Continue pouring in the oil until the mug is two thirds full.

HANDY HINT! If the dressing separates, the situation can normally be recovered by adding some more mustard or beating furiously with the fork.

Tom says you now have enough dressing for at least two salads. You can adjust the recipe to taste. For the more adventurous a crushed clove of garlic can be added at the end to give the dressing real bite.

Dr Peter Brand

Liberal Democrat-Isle of Wight

Peter appears to be standing by his health credentials as a GP with this vegetarian dish, but he also states that it is not only suitable for militant vegetarians but also for hungry friends who need a savoury dish to finish a(nother) bottle of red wine – this being good for the heart of course!

Baked Aubergines

Slice the aubergine in half, scoop out most of the flesh, cut it up coarsely.

For each aubergine add one slice of fresh bread crumbled, quarter of a raw onion finely chopped and one skinned tomato coarsely chopped. Add one to two ounces of grated or crumbled cheese (especially good with over-active remains of Stilton) a tablespoon of parsley and season to taste.

Bind with egg beaten in Worcester sauce, mix by hand and scoop into the aubergine shells. Cook for twenty minutes in the middle of the top oven of an Aga, finishing for ten minutes on the top shelf.

Christine Russell

Labour-City of Chester

Christine has done well in combining some different flavours in this dish which is both a quick and tasty supper meal.

Vegetable Au Gratin
Serves 4

Ingredients:

25g (1oz) butter
1 tablespoon oil
1 onion, chopped/2-3 cloves garlic
1 red pepper, chopped,
3 courgettes sliced
14oz can chopped tomatoes
2 tablespoons tomato puree
salt and freshly ground pepper
250g (8oz) English Brie, cut into cubes
To garnish: sprig of chervil or chopped herbs

Method:

Heat the butter and oil, add the onion, garlic, pepper and courgettes and cook for 4-5 minutes until soft.

Add the tomatoes, tomato puree and seasoning. Cover and simmer gently for 10-12 minutes.

Transfer to an ovenproof dish and top with the English Brie. Place under a pre-heated moderate grill for 2-3 minutes, until the cheese melts. Garnish with a sprig of chervil or sprinkle with herbs. Serve immediately with crusty bread and salad.

Cooking time 15-20 minutes

Brian White

Labour-Milton Keynes North East

Brian has not said so, but we have a feeling this dish is heavily influenced by his wife, Leena, or else his travels as a member of HM Customs and Excise took him to such Nordic areas!

Finnish Swede Casserole
Serves 4-6

Ingredients:

Approx 1kg swedes
Water, salt
2 tablespoon of breadcrumbs
150ml double cream
2 small eggs
approx 100ml syrup
salt, white pepper
(ground) nutmeg

Method:

Peel and cut the swedes into cubes. Boil them until soft in salty water. Mix the breadcrumbs into the cream. Mash the boiled swedes and mix them with the cream/breadcrumb mix. Add the eggs and the spices. Pour the mixture into an ovenproof dish and spread a layer of breadcrumbs on top. Cook in the oven at 175°C for approx one hour. Serving suggestion: A wonderful vegetarian dish on its own, but readers may be interested to learn that this is an essential part of a Finnish Christmas dinner and is served as a vegetable dish with the traditional gammon, boiled potatoes, carrot casserole, white sauce and a traditional salad called 'rosolli'.

Debra Shipley

Labour–Stourbridge

This recipe looks the definite one for MPs returning to empty flats after some time away and discovering what remains are left that could be concocted into something edible!

Chop and Chuck Sauce

Open fridge – chuck in bin anything mouldy.

Chop up anything not lined with fluffy blue coating. Good candidates include:

Ingredients:

Onions, carrots, spinach, garlic, tomatoes, red peppers.

Method:

Heat a few tablespoons of olive oil in a saucepan then chuck in all chopped stuff.

Sweat (nasty but necessary) for five minutes.

Add a tin of chopped tomatoes and tin of butterbeans.

Simmer until you want to eat (25 minutes)

Add salt if you want.

Serve with jacket potato/rice/couscous/bread – or gobble up out of the pan!

Paul Goggins

Labour-Wythenshawe and Sale East

This is one of Paul's favourite pasta recipes, handed down to a friend by the owner of a village restaurant in Italy – only because she lived in England and was therefore unlikely to share it with other restaurants in the area.

Pepper Sauce for Pasta

Ingredients:

1 red pepper
1 green pepper
1 yellow pepper
2 medium sized courgettes
olive oil
Pasta

Method:

Remove the stalks and cores from the peppers, and chop into small pieces. Cut the courgettes into quarters (lengthways) and then slice. Heat the olive oil gently in a pan and add the peppers. Cook over a gentle heat until they are soft. Add the courgettes and continue to heat. Ideally you should then let the vegetables and oil simmer for about one hour – you may need to top up with more oil. The longer you cook it the better.

Serve with your favourite pasta – Paul says it goes down well with spaghetti, or pasta shells, and a good bottle of Italian red wine.

Norman Baker

Liberal Democrat-Lewes

Norman has stormed almost into beating Tony Banks' record for asking more questions in the House than any other MP, even in the short time since his arrival. His list of ingredients will leave you breathless too – but the end result is well worth it!

Lewes Veggie Korma

Korma Ingredients:

Cashew nuts, 1 onion, 2 cloves garlic, 2 bananas, 1 mooli (giant white radish, 1 carrot, 1 small parsnip, half pound mushrooms, root fennel, 1 can chick peas, quarter pint single cream, 2cm block creamed coconut, 1 pint vegetable stock.

Spices for sauce:

6 fresh garlic cloves, 4 pieces cinnamon bark, 1 teaspoon ground coriander, quarter teaspoon ground cumin, 1 teaspoon tumeric, 1 teaspoon ground cinnamon, half teaspoon ground fennel seeds, 2 teaspoons garam masala, quarter teaspoon white mustard seeds.

Ingredients for Potatoes:

3 medium potatoes, quarter onion, 2 cloves garlic, quarter fresh green chilli, vegetable oil, 1 teaspoon garam masala.

Preparation of potatoes:

Chop potatoes into 1 cm cubes. Chop onion garlic and chilli. Heat oil in wok and coat potato cubes with oil. Add onion, garlic chilli and spices. Lower heat and allow to steam for 10 minutes with lid on. Remove lid. Turn up heat and let potatoes become crispy. Drain on kitchen paper.

Preparation of vegetables for Korma:

Chop onion and garlic finely. Slice mushrooms. Puree bananas.

Chop parsnip, mooli and carrot into matchsticks. Chop 2 tablsp of root fennel.

Preparation of Korma sauce:

Heat 4 tablespoons vegetable oil and add cloves of garlic, mustard seeds and cinnamon bark. Fry for 15 seconds. Lower heat slightly and add onion, garlic and root fennel. Fry for 10 minutes until well browned, add mushrooms and fry until they wilt. Add bananas. Prepare vegetable stock in measuring jug. Stir coconut block into stock until it dissolves. Add this to the pan. Gently add cream, then tumeric, coriander, cinnamon, cumin and fennel. Stir gently.

Finally: Add parsnip, mooli and carrot. Stir. Add previously prepared potatoes and chick peas. Cover pan and simmer for 15 minutes or so. Before serving add a handful of cashews and sultanas.

Ben Bradshaw

Labour-Exeter

The former journalist who reported the fall of the Berlin Wall for BBC Radio, here turns to a popular haunt of Italy where he has chosen a pasta dish that combines speed and deliciousness! A healthy meal in little over 10 minutes – no longer to make than the pasta takes to boil.

Pasta Con Salvia

Ingredients:

Pasta (preferably spaghetti or rigatoni)

Garlic, Olive oil & Butter

Fresh sage (preferably from the garden – easy to grow and prolific)

Fresh Parmesan (Must be 'Reggiano' not some cheap imitation)

Salt, Freshly ground black pepper

Method:

While the salted pasta water is heating up, prepare plenty of sage leaves and chopped (never crushed) garlic. Grate (finely) plenty of Parmesan. When the water starts boiling add the pasta. Add the sage and garlic to a little butter and olive oil and a sprinkling of salt and warm gently in another pan. The garlic should go golden brown and the sage very gooey and shrivelled up in a few minutes. When the pasta is ready drain and add the butter, oil, garlic and sage mixture and mix in well. Add the fresh Parmesan and keep mixing. You shouldn't need any more salt. Add black pepper to taste.

Best with red wine and a crispy green salad.

Chris Pond

Labour-Gravesham

Chris, who as well as being involved in the past with the Low Pay Unit, has spent time since his arrival also training to run in the London Marathon. These are just the healthy thing he needs for his diet – though he sneakily suggests adding them to a roast meat joint or other roasted vegetables!

Green Beans

Slice two medium sized onions into rings and fry in a large saucepan with a generous slug of olive oil. Let the oil start to burn but not the onion – it's a good trick if you can pull it off. While all that is happening drop in as many chopped cloves of garlic as your friends will tolerate without avoiding your company later. Add a spoonful of Provencal herbs. Now just add all the green beans, stirring them until they are soft, but not mushy. Finally add a tin of tomatoes stirring them in with the beans and onions. Since tinned tomatoes can be bitter I add a teaspoon of sugar, but that is optional. Allow the beans to simmer gently for 5- 10 minutes or as long as you like. As long as they don't dry out, they're better the longer they stew. Chris says he cheats by using frozen green beans – they taste as good and after hours of 'topping and tailing' letters, he doesn't want to spend time doing it to beans as well!

Alan Johnson

Labour-Hull West and Hessle

Alan was delighted that the chosen charity of co-author Nick Palmer was the Cats Protection League as he also has two rescued cats – both black and white, which is entirely fitting for an ex-postman like himself! Alan's chosen recipe is one which he considers to be his biggest culinary success to date and was taken from the Sainsbury's Book of Vegetarian Suppers. He dedicates it to his two glorious cats, Jake and Lou-Lou.

Vegetable Paella

Ingredients:

4 tablespoons oil

2 cloves garlic, crushed/1 large onion, sliced

4 celery sticks, sliced

1 teaspoon paprika

1 each red, green and yellow pepper, cored, seeded and cut into squares

125g (4oz) whole green beans

350g (12oz) Italian risotto rice

397g (14oz) can peeled tomatoes

2 pinches saffron strands

900ml (one and a half pints) vegetable stock

397g (14oz) can artichoke hearts, drained and halved

125g (2 oz) pitted black olives

1 tablespoon lemon juice

2 tablespoons chopped parsley

Salt and pepper to taste

lemon wedges and parsley to garnish

Method:

Heat the oil in a pan, add the garlic, onion and celery and saute until the onion is transparent. Add the paprika, peppers and beans and sauté for 2-3 minutes, stirring constantly. Add the rice and cook for 2 minutes still stirring constantly. Add the tomatoes with their juice, saffron and stock and simmer gently for 15-20 minutes, stirring frequently, until almost all the liquid has been absorbed. Add the remaining ingredients and heat gently for about 5 minutes. Garnish with lemon wedges and parsley to serve.

Needs nothing more than some crusty bread and perhaps a lightly chilled Gewürztraminer!

David Drew

Labour/Co-Op-Stroud

David's wife sent in examples from a cookbook compiled by herself and a friend a few years ago – it appears to include contributions from all the members of the Drew family, including the children with some delightful drawings and handy hints.

Choux Pastry with Ratatouille

Ingredients:

Choux Pastry

2oz (50g) margarine

Salt and pepper

2 size 3 eggs, beaten

5fl oz (150ml) water

3oz (75g) plain flour

3oz mature Cheddar

Ratatouille

1 tablespoon olive oil

1 aubergine

1 medium green pepper

14oz tin tomatoes

1 tablespoon chopped fresh basil *or* 1 teaspoon dried basil

(optional) 1 large onion

3 small courgettes

1 medium red pepper

2 tablespoons tomato puree	
quarter pint vegetable stock	
grated cheese to garnish	

Method for the choux pastry:

Put the margarine water and a pinch of salt in a large pan. Have the flour ready on a small plate nearby. Bring the margarine and water to a fast boil then draw the pan off the heat and tip the flour in all at once. Beat briskly with a wooden spoon until the mixture forms a ball that rolls cleanly around the pan. Leave to cool for 5 minutes. Slowly add the beaten egg a little at a time beating well between each addition (This can be done with an electric mixer) Grate the cheese and add to the mixture. Grease a baking tray and place heaped adjoining teaspoons to form a 10 inch circle. Bake in a preheated oven at 220°C/425°F/ Gas Mark 7 for about 40 minutes until the choux pastry is puffy and brown.

Method for the Ratatouille:

Heat the oil in a pan and fry the onion gently without browning. Add the aubergine, courgettes and peppers and fry gently for about 10 minutes. Stir in the tomatoes, tomato puree and vegetable stock. Cover the pan and simmer gently for a further 15 minutes, stirring occasionally. Stir in the basil and season to taste. Transfer the hot choux pastry ring to a heated platter and spoon on the ratatouille filling.

Serve immediately sprinkled with grated cheese.

Linda Gilroy

Labour/Co-Op-Plymouth Sutton

Linda was previously a Regional Manager of the Gas Consumer's Council and mentions 'energy' as one of her special interests. This quick fiery red recipe should certainly give you some well needed energy!

Stuffed Red Peppers

Ingredients:

4 red peppers

200 grams cooked rice

2-3oz mushrooms, chopped

1 onion (largish) chopped

1 tin Campbell's Italian tomato soup (condensed)

1 tablespoon olive oil

Methods:

Slice top off the red peppers and keep. Boil 2-3 pints water. Cover red peppers with boiled water and leave for 10 minutes. Heat oil in deep frying pan. Saute onions, add mushrooms and rice. Add condensed soup (and fresh herbs if available). Fill red peppers with mixture and cover with tops. Bake in oven 180°- 200°C for 40 minutes. Serve with green salad. May be frozen and reheated in microwave.

Section Six

Desserts and Baking *or* Adjournment
debates/towards recess

Desserts and Baking *or* Adjournment debates/towards recess

Adjournments do not just mean the end of the session or of the working day for MPs. Adjournment debates allow MPs the opportunity to raise a subject of his or her choice and to receive an answer from a Minister in the relevant Government department. These can happen on a daily basis, but also a second type of adjournment debate can be taken on a Wednesday morning when topics can be those selected by committees. There are also more general topical debates which are debated on the Wednesday before a holiday recess.

Some adjournment debates can also be initiated by the government. And finally should an emergency adjournment debate be called – this might cover a subject suddenly to come to the attention of MPs often on a national or international subject, rather than constituency related – it can often be disconcerting for MPs when a subject of incredible importance for them is greeted by a virtually empty chamber, but often these debates provide an entertaining, informative and welcome conclusion to the more staged packed heated debates. To sweeten all MPs up as the afternoon session in particular flows on, tea and a sweet treat or cake on the terrace may be just the order of the day!

Vernon Coaker

Labour-Gedling

Vernon lists the environment as one of his special interests, so a healthy walk out to collect some fresh ingredients for this delicious recipe is obviously a good idea!

Blackberry Pie

Ingredients:

Short Pastry
200 grams plain flour
pinch of salt
100 grams of margarine
2 tablespoons of cold water
1 dessert spoon of sugar to sprinkle on top of pastry

Contents:

750 grams of stewed blackberries with sugar as necessary

Method:

Wash and stew the blackberries with small amount of water and sugar.

Cut up margarine into pieces in large bowl.

Sieve flour into large bowl with pinch of salt. Rub in, until you have a breadcrumbs consistency.

Add water until of consistency to roll out on floured board.

Cut pastry to pie dish. Fill with stewed blackberries. Cover with layer of pastry and sprinkle with sugar.

Bake in moderate oven, gas mark 6, for approx 25 minutes until golden brown.

Rosemary McKenna

Labour–Cumbernauld and Kilsyth

The Italian theme very popular in many MP's savoury recipes has followed us to the dessert trolley with this delicious pudding from Rosemary.

Tiramisu
Serves 6

Ingredients:

4 eggs – separated
4 tablespoons icing sugar
3 tablespoons brandy
500g/18oz mascarpone cheese
18 boudoir biscuits
285ml/half pint strong freshly made coffee, cooled
3 tablespoons cocoa powder

Method:

Whisk the egg yolks with the sugar until pale and fluffy, then whisk in the brandy and cheese.

Whisk the egg whites until very stiff and fold into the cheese mixture. Spread one third of the cheese mixture over the bottom of the bowl. Cover with layers of biscuits dipping each one in coffee first. Break them in half if necessary to fit the corners. Spread another third of the cheese mixture over the biscuits. Cover with remaining biscuits and finish with remaining cheese mixture. Smooth the top.

Chill for a few hours. Before serving sprinkle with cocoa.

Alasdair Morgan

SNP–Galloway and Upper Nithsdale

Alasdair has a delightful alcohol filled concoction here that is definitely regionally inspired.

Flummery Drambuie

Ingredients:

4 egg yolks

3 tablespoons caster sugar

3 tablespoons Drambuie

7 and a half fl oz double cream

Method:

Put the egg yolks and sugar into a bowl which will fit over a saucepan of simmering water. Using a rotary beater, quickly whip together the eggs and sugar. When the mixture thickens and has increased in volume add the Drambuie. Continue beating until the mixture is stiff and will stand in peaks. Whip the cream until it is semi-stiff and fold it in gently. Pour the flummery into wide champagne glasses or shallow glass dishes and chill. Before serving the top of each can be decorated with a piped rosette of whipped cream.

Jackie Ballard

Liberal Democrat–Taunton

Jackie does not consider herself much of an active cook these days, but as she was promoted to the Catering Committee she felt it was incumbent on her to provide a recipe! This then is one she assures us she occasionally assembles with her own fair hands. It is fattening, very alcoholic and probably something which should be avoided by any MP who wants to stay alive until the next election!

Ginger Roll

Ingredients:

1 packet ginger nut biscuits
1 large carton double cream
a bottle of brandy (probably a quarter bottle will do!)
1 Cadbury's flake

Method:

Pour the brandy into a shallow dish, whip the double cream until fairly stiff. Dunk the biscuits in the brandy, not so much that they disintegrate but enough for them to be pleasantly damp. Sandwich each biscuit together with the cream and assemble into cylindrical shape. When you have finished the biscuits drink the remaining brandy! Cover the cylinder with the double cream, not forgetting the ends of the cylinder. Crumble the flake over the top and serve, to gasps of delight!

Fiona MacTaggart

Labour-Slough

This is a quite different idea that will turn the loveliest of fruit into pure delight!

Fried Nectarines
Serves 4

Split 4 nectarines in half and remove stones. Fry them in 1oz butter scattering a rounded dessertspoon of brown sugar over. Turn them over in the pan and when the butter and sugar mixture is getting bubbly add the juice of half an orange and half a lemon.

Continue to cook until nectarines are cooked through (about 3 minutes) and the sauce is quite reduced.

For a special occasion you can flambé these before serving by warming a little brandy in a ladle and then setting it on fire and pouring over the fruit.

Serve immediately with thick natural yoghurt.

Michael Moore

Liberal Democrat-Tweedale, Ettrick & Lauderdale

Michael says the length of preparation and cooking time are well worth it – although he says kids love it because it's so puddingy! we have no doubt this is one that regularly appears on the menus in the Westminster Restaurants!

Bread Pudding
Serves 6-8

Ingredients:

1 large (stale) loaf – sliced
6-8ozs butter or margarine
Boiling water
Two handfuls dried fruit – raisins, currants, sultanas or mixed
1 large Bramley apple
6-8ozs sugar – demerara is best!

Method:

Arrange bread slices in large bowl. Pour on enough boiling water to soak through and make bread thoroughly wet – best to work it in by hand or a large fork at this stage. Pour away any excess water and add butter or margarine. The warmth of the bread will begin to melt it in, but fork fat well into the damp bread and then add the sugar. Mix all together now with a large wooden spoon and add dried fruit. (Glace cherries may also be added to make this a bit special!). Peel and chop the Bramley apple and mix that in. You may also wish to add a little grated rind of orange at this stage and/or orange juice. Grease a small roasting tin (for a deep pudding) or a large roasting tin(for a shallow pudding) and bake in a moderate to hot oven (gas Mark 6) for around 40-60 minutes

– check it! Some families like it crispy around the edges. When cooked, remove. Whilst still warm you may like to pour over a little more orange juice and grated rind, mixed with brown sugar – this gives a wonderful tangy caramalised topping! May be served with cream, custard, ice-cream or alone. Delicious hot or cold, but slices best cold and may be safely re-heated.

Janet Dean

Labour-Burton

Janet has apologised for being an oldie who still works in imperial measurements in her cooking but as many others clearly still think in the same way we feel sure she can be excused and also congratulated for this tangy sweet!

Lemon Cheesecake

Ingredients:

8oz digestive biscuits
4oz margarine
8oz cottage cheese
Half a pack of lemon jelly
4oz cream
1 teaspoon of sugar
5 fl oz boiling water

Method:

Melt the margarine and add to the crushed digestive biscuits. Line a shallow cake/flan dish with the mixture.

Melt the jelly in the boiling water and allow to cool. Sieve the cottage cheese and whisk the cream.

Add the cottage cheese, cream and cooled jelly together, and whisk until smooth. Pour onto the base and allow to set in a fridge.

Add preferred fruit either before or after the mixture is put onto the base, or serve plain.

Diana Organ

Labour-Forest of Dean

Diana has chosen a pudding that is a firm favourite with her daughters, Lucy and Daisy.

Lucy's Chocolate Grape Surprise

Ingredients:

1 medium pot of natural yoghurt
1 medium pot of creme fraiche
1lb big seedless green grapes
1 large bar dark chocolate

Method:

Mix the yoghurt and creme fraiche together in a mixing bowl.

Halve all the grapes. Grate the chocolate. Take a large glass bowl and put a layer of the yoghurt mixture in the bowl; cover with the halved grapes, then a layer of grated chocolate.

Continue to layer the ingredients until the bowl is full ending with a layer of grated chocolate.

Put in the fridge to chill for at least half an hour.

Julie Kirkbride

Conservative-Bromsgrove

Over the years Julie has worked extensively in current affairs on the television and in the newspapers so this was no doubt useful as a quick and delicious pudding. Julie's comment on it is 'YUM YUM!'

Apple Rapture

Ingredients:

Cooking apples (amount depending on size of dish)

Sour cream

Demerara sugar

Method:

Stew cooking apples, which can then be used either hot or cold. Cover a flameproof dish with the stewed apple. Pour over the top sufficient sour cream to cover the apple.

Then sprinkle demerara sugar over the top of that and grill mixture under a high heat until the sugar has melted and caramalised.

Doug Naysmith

Labour/Co-Op-Bristol North West

Having spent much of his working life prior to being elected as a researcher in laboratories studying immunology. Doug has given us a highly healthy recipe with which to end any meal.

Oatmeal and Yoghurt Cream
Serves 4

Ingredients:

40g blanched almonds finely chopped (or flaked almonds crumbled)

40g medium oatmeal (or porridge oats)

25g muscovado sugar

grated rind and juice of half a lemon

150g natural low fat yoghurt 150ml double cream, whipped

1 tablespoon flaked almonds, toasted

Method:

Mix together the chopped almonds and oatmeal. Spread on a baking sheet and place under a pre-heated hot grill for about 2 minutes, stirring frequently to brown evenly. Leave to cool.

Mix sugar with the lemon rind and juice. Stir into the yoghurt with the almond mixture then fold in the cream. Spoon into individual glass dishes (if wished) and chill until required. Decorate with the flaked toasted almonds to serve.

Colin Breed

Liberal Democrat-Cornwall South East

As Colin is a banker by profession we just wonder who decided to call this naughty but nice chocolate dessert by such an unglamorous name? Doesn't quite seem to do it justice!

Colin's Chocolate Goo

Ingredients:

8oz chocolate (melted)
4 eggs
Half oz butter
1 tablespoon dark rum

Method:

Melt chocolate – add 4 egg yolks (beaten), add butter and rum. Mix together. Beat egg whites until stiff and then fold into chocolate mixture. Put into serving bowl or individual glasses and chill in fridge.

Dr Rudi Vis

Labour-Finchley and Golders Green

The usual image of chestnuts is of cold winter nights and the nuts being roasted outside. But the puree itself is a very tasty option for many recipes, and here Rudi has submitted the following which is a frequent production in his home.

Chestnut Dessert

Ingredients:

1lb tin of chestnut puree
5oz unsalted butter
5oz icing sugar
1 egg yolk
2 packets sponge fingers
Vanilla essence
Half pint double strength coffee (cooled)

Method:

Beat the butter, sugar, chestnut puree and egg yolk with a few drops of vanilla to a smooth cream. Dip sponge fingers very quickly one at a time into coffee and line a pudding basin with them. Place half the chestnut cream mixture into the basin over the bottom section of the sponge fingers. Add another layer of coffee dipped sponge fingers followed by remaining chestnut cream mixture.

Place a plate on top and weigh it down with something heavy (a weeks *Hansard* works well!). Leave for 10 hours in fridge.

To serve: Run a palette knife around the edge of the pudding, invert a plate on top and tip upside down. Serve with single (unwhipped) cream.

This pudding can be frozen. Remember that the very young, elderly and pregnant women should avoid raw eggs.

Jackie Lawrence

Labour-Preseli Pembrokeshire

Jackie says this is an impressive but very simple dessert, but warns – don't eat too much – it's full of calories!

Banoffee Pie

Ingredients:

1 large packet of digestive biscuits
1 can condensed milk
3 bananas whipping cream
1oz butter

Method:

Simmer the can of condensed milk in a pan of water for one and a half hours on a low heat (do not pierce the can). Place digestive biscuits in a clean polythene bag and break into pieces. When broken into small pieces roll bag with rolling pin to break into fine crumbs.

Melt butter in pan and add biscuit crumbs. Use biscuits to form pie base in a flan tin and place in fridge till cool. Slice bananas lengthways and place on top of biscuit base. When condensed milk has cooled but is still slightly warm open tin and spoon contents over the sliced bananas. Whip cream and add to top of condensed milk when fully cooked.

Yvette Cooper

Labour-Pontefract and Castleford

Yvette says this is the perfect recipe for the person that has just spent two hours trying to light a barbecue, eaten a couple of burnt and blackened sausages, and now wants something extremely easy for dessert. Can we expect this to appear on the Chancellor's BBQ at Number 11, perhaps assisted by Yvette's husband, Ed Balls? Certainly one that is economical with its ingredients! A very prudent pudding!

Barbecued Bananas

Ingredients:

1 banana

1 bar of plain or milk chocolate (whichever you prefer)

Method:

Simply make an incision down the length of the banana and stuff pieces of chocolate into the middle. Press the banana skin back together again and place on the barbecue. You can also wrap the banana in foil and place it straight onto the coals. Cooking time varies depending on the heat of the barbecue but you'll know it's ready when you open the banana to find that it has gone soft, the chocolate's melted and you're left with one sweet, gooey and delicious mess! (For extra calories serve with ice-cream)

Anne Campbell

Labour–Cambridge

Anne's recipe was passed onto her by a friend. It's quick and easy to make and makes good use of fresh fruit even in the depths of winter. It's refreshing, but not too sharp and can be adapted to suit whatever fruit is available.

Citrus Fruit Brulé

Ingredients:

1 ordinary grapefruit
1 pink grapefruit or a combination of any of these: 2 oranges/3 clementines
Quarter pint double cream
Quarter pint soured cream
2oz caster sugar
3oz muscovado sugar
Generous squeeze of lemon juice

Method:

Prepare the fruit by peeling the grapefruit and paring the skin from each segment. Peel the oranges, remove all the pith and membrane then slice them across into rounds about a quarter inch thick. Peel the clementines. Halve the grapefruit segments and orange slices if they are very large and leave the clementine segments whole. Place all the fruit in a flameproof shallow serving dish and spread out evenly. Whip both the creams together with the caster sugar and lemon juice and spread over the fruit. Crumble the muscovado sugar and sprinkle it thickly over the surface. Preheat the grill to full for a few minutes then place the dish under the grill, at least two and a half inches from the source of the heat. Keep turning the dish until the sugar becomes hot and bubbling (this will take about one and a half minutes). Allow to cool and chill in fridge until required.

Robert Syms

Conservative-Poole

Super poem accompanies this recipe:

> Home from the House,
> Friends coming to eat,
> Joint in the oven,
> Now what for a sweet?
>> *Try this*

Baked Peaches

Ingredients:

4 fresh peaches
Half cup light sugar syrup
4 tablespoons mincemeat
4 tablespoons brandy

Method:

Skin peaches by immersing in boiling water for a few minutes, and remove stone. Slice in half and place in an ovenproof dish. Fill centres with mincemeat. Pour syrup around base of peaches.

Spoon brandy over the top of the peaches and bake in the oven (moderate) for about 25 minutes until cooked. Serve with creme fraiche or cream.

This recipe is just as good using a large tin of peach halves.

Candy Atherton

Labour–Falmouth and Camborne

A very gingery recipe to tickle the taste buds!

Ginger Cream Log

Ingredients:

8oz ginger biscuits
8oz double cream
1 cup sherry
Crystallised ginger cut in small pieces and/or walnuts for decoration

Method:

Whip cream until stiff. Dip biscuits one at a time in sherry. Cover with cream and sandwich together. Use the whole packet and cover completely with cream. Decorate with crystallised ginger and/or walnuts if liked. Place in fridge for two hours before serving.

Graham Brady

Conservative-Altrincham and Sale West

Graham has not just taken the whole credit for this recipe, but says it is submitted by his whole family. It seems a good one for the children!

Brownies with hot fudge sauce
Serves 8

Ingredients:

250g unsalted butter
100g plain flour
250g dark chocolate, chopped
50g self-raising flour
550g caster sugar
50g cocoa powder
5 eggs
50g dark chocolate (extra)
1 teaspoon vanilla essence

Hot fudge sauce:

125ml cream
150g dark chocolate, chopped
50g white marshmallows, chopped

Method:

Brownies: Grease 20cm x 30cm baking tray, cover base and sides with baking paper. Combine butter and chocolate in medium pan and stir over low heat until smooth. Transfer to large bowl. Stir in sugar then eggs and essence, then sifted flours and cocoa and extra chocolate. Pour mixture into prepared tray. Bake in moderate oven for about 45 minutes or until firm. Cool in tray. Refrigerate until cold. Turn brownie onto board and trim edges. Cut into quarters, cut each quarter into half diagonally, cut each triangle in half. Serve brownies with ice-cream and hot fudge sauce.

Hot fudge sauce: Combine all ingredients in small pan. Stir over heat without boiling until smooth.

Bev Hughes

Labour-Stretford & Urmston

Bev says this dessert is easy to make but looks spectacular! It is basically two large rounds of meringue with a filling of creme patisserie and pureed fruit. Any fresh or canned fruit will be fine although something slightly tart such as apricots counter balances the sweet creme.

Sweet Nothing

Ingredients:

Meringue:

4 large egg whites
6oz caster sugar
1 level teaspoon cornflour
Half teaspoon vinegar

Creme:

4 large egg yolks
Three quarters pint milk
Vanilla essence
4oz caster sugar
1oz cornflour in 3 tablespoons milk

Fruit:

Tin pf apricots in natural juice, or
other similar canned or fresh fruit

Method:

Oil 2 baking sheets, line with silicone paper and oil that lightly.
Preheat oven to 150°C (300°F). Put egg whites in a large clean
bowl and whisk until they form stiff peaks (which don't slide
when the bowl is tipped. Don't overbeat). Add the caster sugar an
ounce at a time, whisking well in between. Whisk in the vinegar
and sieved cornflour. Divide into two and make two large circles
of meringue, one on each baking sheet (Adjust the size to fit the
plate or serving dish you are going to use.) Place in oven, turn
heat down to 140°C (275°F) and cook for an hour. Turn off oven
and leave until cold or overnight if convenient.

Creme and fruit: Beat egg yolks well in a bowl. Add sugar and
milk to non-stick pan and bring just to boiling point. Pour over
egg yolks beating all the time. Beat well. Return mixture to pan,
add dissolved cornflour and vanilla essence, bring slowly to heat
stirring with a wooden spoon. Allow to col. Drain fruit if canned.
Puree in liquidiser or through sieve.

Assemble by placing one layer of meringue bottom-up on a flat
plate (or round dish with a small edge) Spread a layer of cold
creme then a layer of pureed fruit. Add the second meringue layer,
top side up and dust with icing sugar.

Phil Hope

Labour/Co-Op-Corby

Let the recipe speak for itself!

New Labour Cheesecake

The Description:

Like the new Labour Government this cheesecake
- is built upon a delicious sponge foundation of traditional Labour values,
- embodies a substantial texture of cream and cheese policy directly relevant to the needs and tastes of people in the new millennium,
- is filled with flavoursome sultanas that burst excitingly upon the palate like Labour's many new projects and initiatives,
- gives a sharp lemony tang of continuous campaigning zeal,
- and, to cap it all, has a sweet and crunchy topping that will have people crying out for a second or even a third helping or term of office.

The Ingredients:

1lb curd cheese
6oz castor sugar
Half lemon (juice)
4 egg yolks
4 beaten egg whites until stiff
5oz double cream
1 packet trifle sponges
3 tablespoons sultanas

The Method:

Cut sugary tops off the trifle sponges thinly, chop and reserve. Slice sponges in half to make them thinner. Layer base of deep tin with removable base. Mix cheese, caster sugar, lemon juice, cream, egg yolks and sultanas. Add whipped egg whites folding gently. Pour mixture onto sponge base. Sprinkle chopped sugary bits on top. Cook in oven at gas mark 4 for 45 minutes.

Leave to cool and then place in fridge to chill.

Ivan Lewis

Labour-Bury South

Simple but super – sums up this firm favourite.

Ivan's Apple Crumble

Ingredients:

One and a half lbs of sliced baking apples (cored and peeled)

8oz plain flour

2oz margarine

2oz sugar

2oz sultanas

Cinnamon

Method:

Place sliced apples, sultanas, 1oz sugar cinnamon (to taste) in pie dish. Rub together flour and margarine until like breadcrumbs. Mix in 1oz of sugar and place on top of fruit.

Bake in oven 200°/400°F gas mark 6 for 25 minutes.

Baking

Phil Sawford

Labour-Kettering

Phil says this carrot cake is always popular at his fund-raising events – a definite bonus for any local political party. Readers will find three different types of carrot cake within this baking section so obviously it is up to you to decide your favourite – it certainly means our MPs are trying their best to put a good healthy 'spin' on fattening cakes in general!

A Hint of Red Cake

Ingredients:

150g sugar

3 eggs

175ml corn oil

1x 5ml vanilla flavouring

100g walnut pieces

250g carrots

150g self-raising flour

1 teaspoon cinnamon

1 teaspoon salt

Icing:

85g full-fat soft cream cheese

50g butter

100g icing sugar

walnut halves to decorate

Method:

Pre-heat oven (180°C 350°F Gas mark 4) Prepare 22cm round tin, line with greaseproof paper, and grease.

Mix corn oil, sugar eggs and flavouring well in a bowl. Wash and peel the carrots, cut in small pieces. Add to the mixture with flour, cinnamon and salt. Mix well in blender, then add the chopped walnuts. Bake for approx 1 hr 15 mins.

Icing: Mix the cream cheese, butter and icing sugar together. Cover cake with the mixture and decorate with walnut halves.

Dr Evan Harris

Liberal Democrat-Oxford West & Abingdon

Evan notices that MPs often say they are too busy to eat properly. For him nothing is further from the truth. If anything he feels MPs are too busy to exercise properly. His previous job was as a junior hospital doctor, where standard practice for nights on call was to order from the local 'Chinese' (the hospital had very poor catering facilities after 6pm when the last manager went home!). Often, however the Chinese meal was devoured three hours later when there was a break in the hectic proceedings. One of the first things he did when elected was to eat Chinese food while it was still hot! But for us he has an 'old standby' – not his mother herself but one of her recipes!

Summer Sponge Cake with fruit and cheese filling

Ingredients:

4 eggs, separated
5oz flour
6oz castor sugar
2 tablespoon orange juice
5 tablespoon sunflower oil
1 teaspoon salt
1lb fromage frais
Half cup milk
1 tin fruit in natural juices
1 sachet vanilla pudding

Method:

Whisk egg whites with pinch of salt until they form stiff peaks. Add half castor sugar and beat until mixture is thick and glossy. Blend egg yolks, oil, sugar and orange juice. Add flour and beat until mixture is pale and creamy. Fold meringue into mixture until well blended. Turn into a 9 inch round greased and floured cake tin. Bake in moderate oven at gas mark 4, 180°C for 30 minutes until pale and golden and a skewer comes out of cake clean. Leave to cool and slide out of cake tin. Prepare filling by placing fromage frais, vanilla pudding and milk into bowl, mix well until thoroughly blended. Split cake, spread with cheese filling and drained fruit. Dust top of cake with icing sugar. Refrigerate until required.

Stephen Hepburn

Labour-Jarrow

Stephen has done us proud with his own original and special Christmas Cake recipe. His Christmas Day pig-out is never complete without a slice!

Stephen's Special Christmas Cake

Ingredients:

10oz Self-raising flour
Pinch of salt
1 teaspoon mixed spice
2oz ground almonds
6oz of butter or margarine
1 and a quarter pounds mixed dried fruit
4oz chopped almonds/hazelnuts/Brazil nuts
6oz chopped glazed cherries
3 large free range eggs
1 tablespoon golden treacle
4 tablespoons House of Commons whisky
2 tablespoons skimmed milk

Method:

In a separate bowl place flour, salt, mixed spice and ground almonds together and mix thoroughly. Begin by creaming the butter/margarine together until the mixture is light and fluffy. Stir in the tablespoon of warmed golden treacle. Whisk the first egg and place it in the bowl with the butter and sugar and add two tablespoons of dried ingredients, flour etc and beat thoroughly. Whisk the second egg and add to the mixture two more tablespoons of the dried ingredients and beat thoroughly. Whisk the third egg and repeat.

After beating the mixture together thoroughly add the House of Commons whisky. When this is thoroughly blended add the milk and blend together. Fold in the remaining dried ingredients very gently. Add to the mixture the chopped nuts and cherries but be careful not to beat the mixture. Bake in a lined 8 inch square tin for 1 hour on gas mark 4, and 2 hours on gas mark 1 on the middle shelf. When the cake is cold it can now be wrapped in tin foil. Place in a large tin with a secure lid. Place an apple in the tin with the cake to keep the cake wonderfully moist. Leave in the tin for at least one month and then prepare the cake with marzipan and icing and Christmas novelties.

Stephen Pound

Labour–Ealing North

These are some tasty biscuits that are his children's favourite and are a recipe that came from their Grandpa.

Brumpa's Biscuits

Ingredients:

6oz margarine
1 tablespoon golden syrup
1 breakfast cup of granulated sugar
1 breakfast cup of plain white flour
1 breakfast cup of oats
1 teaspoon baking powder
1 teaspoon of bicarbonate of soda

Method:

In a pan melt the margarine syrup and sugar over a low heat until dissolved.

In a bowl mix the dry ingredients-flour oats baking powder and bicarbonate of soda. Make a well in the centre of the dry ingredients and pour in the melted fats and sugars and mix thoroughly.

Drop teaspoons of the mixture onto a greased baking tray. When you have used all the mixture place the tray of biscuits in the oven for 1 hour or until golden brown on Gas Mark 1, 275°F, 100°C. Reduce the cooking time slightly if you have a fan assisted oven, but check to see if they are golden.

Donald Gorrie

Liberal Democrat-Edinburgh West

Donald says he is rather afraid of cooking, but his wife makes marvellous oatcakes which he says are enthused over by all his visitors.

Astrid's Oatcakes

Ingredients:

2 teaspoons of medium oatmeal
Half teaspoon bicarbonate of soda
Quarter teaspoon salt
A knob of melted dripping

Method:

Preheat the oven to 180°C (a fan oven is good), mix all the ingredients in a bowl and then add enough almost boiling water to bind everything together. Don't make the mixture sloppy. Take small quantities at a time, cover with dry oatmeal and roll out very thin. Place on a baking tin and cook for about 20 minutes or until the edges just begin to turn pale brown. To keep them flat turn over half way through the cooking time.

Delicious with butter and marmalade, cheese or honey and easy enough for anyone to make!

Gisela Stuart

Labour–Birmingham Edgbaston

Gisela's constituency was second fastest in conducting election night count. This recipe too is quick but also absolutely delicious, and Gisela says her children absolutely adore it.

Apple Buns

Ingredients:

2 medium sized cooking apples
8oz of wholemeal flour
Pinch of salt
Half teaspoon of ground cinnamon
1 teaspoon of baking powder
6oz butter
2oz of raw brown sugar
1 beaten egg

Method:

Core and dice the apples. Combine flour, salt, spice and baking powder in basin. Rub butter in until mixture resembles fine crumbs. Add remaining ingredients and mix well. Place well formed rounds (egg size) on baking sheet. Bake at 190°C or 375°F for 20–25 minutes until golden brown. Cool slightly on tin before transferring to wire tray for cooling.

Linda Perham

Labour-Ilford North

Linda has offered a recipe that always has people asking her for the recipe at fetes – she has honestly admitted they are from Mary Berry's Bumper Bake-In.

Coffee Triangles

Ingredients:

2oz walnuts
6oz soft margarine
6oz caster sugar
3 eggs
1 tablespoon coffee essence
6oz self-raising flour

Coffee Icing:

8oz icing sugar
3oz soft margarine
3oz milk
1 tablespoon coffee essence

Method:

Grease and base line a 12 x 8 and a half by 2 in tin. Preheat oven to 350°F, 180°C, gas mark 4. Chop walnuts. Place margarine, sugar, eggs and coffee essence in a bowl. Sift in flour and baking powder. Beat until smooth. Stir in walnuts. Spoon mixture into tin. Smooth the top and cook for 35 minutes until well risen and shrinking away from the sides. The cake should spring back when pressed with the finger tips. Cool.

Sift icing sugar into a basin. Add margarine, milk and coffee essence. Beat until smooth. Remove cake from the tin and spread icing over. Just before packing or serving, cut into 3 lengthways. Cut each strip into 4 squares and then cut each square in half diagonally to form 24 triangles.

Derek Twigg

Labour–Halton

Derek's favourite cake recipe is one that is made by his wife Mary. Definitely one for the Westminster tearooms!

Mary's Carrot Cake

Ingredients:

275g plain flour

1 teaspoon bicarbonate of soda

2 teaspoons baking powder

1 teaspoon cinnamon

Pinch of salt

175g light muscovado sugar

75g chopped mixed nuts (optional)

3 size 3 eggs

1 large ripe banana, peeled and mashed

175g finely grated carrots

175ml sunflower oil

Cream Cheese frosting:

115g unsalted butter

115g low fat cream cheese

225g icing sugar

1 tablespoon orange flower water (or orange juice)

Finely grated zest of orange

Method:

Preheat oven to 180°C, 350°F Gas mark 4. Grease a 20 cm round cake tin and line with greaseproof paper.

Sieve together the flour, bicarbonate of soda, baking powder, cinnamon and salt into a bowl, stir in the sugar and nuts. Add the eggs, banana, carrots and oil, beat together for 1 minute until smooth. Pour into the cake tin and level. Bake for 1 hr until a warmed skewer inserted in the centre comes out cleanly. Leave in the tin for 10 mins then turn out to cool.

Make the frosting : soften the butter and cheese together, then beat in the orange flower water (or orange juice) until smooth and fluffy. Cut the cake in half and use a third of the frosting to sandwich together. Spread remainder over the top and sides of the cake, then sprinkle with the orange zest.

Barbara Follett

Labour-Stevenage

The former 'image maker' of the Labour Party, Barbara has designs on our sweet tooth with two mouth-watering recipes. She says they are very popular with her family and friends and the flapjack is entirely her own creation. She suggests it is best served warm.

Chocolate Brownies

Ingredients:

3oz cocoa powder
3oz Cadbury's chocolate break
6oz self-raising flour
18oz flora margarine
18oz soft dark brown sugar
6 eggs

Method:

Whisk margarine and sugar until creamy. Then add the eggs, one at a time. Mix together the chocolate and cocoa and self-raising flour. Add to the butter and egg mixture. Bake in a preheated oven at 190°C or gas mark 5 for 30 minutes.

Flapjacks:

Ingredients:

2 cups margarine
4 tablespoons syrup
2 cups brown sugar

8 cups oats
2 teaspoons salt
2 teaspoons vanilla

Methods:

Preheat oven to gas mark 4 to 6, or electric 180°F to 200°C. Butter cake tins. Melt the margarine, vanilla syrup and brown sugar in a pan. Stir the oats into the mixture. Put into the cake tins and bake for 10–15 minutes.

Andrew Tyrie

Conservative-Chichester

This is a lovely favourite of many and can be used as a pudding too. Andrew suggests serving them hot with a dollop of apple sauce on each square. He also makes use of that lovely word 'goo' again!

Sticky Gingerbread

Ingredients:

6oz butter or margarine
5oz soft, dark brown sugar
8oz black treacle
2 size 2-3 eggs, beaten
9oz self raising flour
1 dessert spoon ground ginger
Half teaspoon bicarbonate of soda
Quarter teaspoon cinnamon
Quarter teaspoon ground cloves
Half teaspoon ground nutmeg
4 tablespoons Guinness

Method:

Light the oven at 180°C (350°F) or gas mark 4. Grease an oblong roasting tin about 10 ins long (8 ins square is OK). Melt butter or margarine, mix in sugar and treacle off the heat, then beaten eggs. Sift flour with dry ingredients, then beat into treacle mixture with a wooden spoon. Mix Guinness with 4 tablespoons hot water, bring to the boil and stir into mixture, which will now be a thick goo that can be poured into the prepared tin. It will rise magically and lighten in the oven in about 40–45 minutes. Cool it in the tin and cut into 12 squares. If you want to make it in advance cover the tin tightly with clingfilm.

Dan Norris

Labour–Wansdyke

A short, but tasty cake recipe that spices up the apples in the mix to tempt the taste buds.

Apple Cake

225g self-raising flour
100g brown sugar
100g butter
350g cooking apples
1 beaten egg
1 teaspoon each of mixed spice and ground cinnamon
Pinch of salt

Method:

Mix together the flour, sugar, salt and spices. Rub in the butter to make a breadcrumb-type consistency. Add beaten egg and chopped apples (peeled and cored) to the mixture. Stir all these ingredients together quickly. Press into a lined and greased baking tin (approx 7 inches square). Bake for approx 35–40 minutes at 190°.

Liz Blackman

Labour-Erewash

Being on the Treasury Select Committee and helping to put together this book, Liz has calculated that this recipe will definitely hit the right mark. She says it is foolproof, and best of all the kids love it. The best recommendation for anything from Mum!

Crunchie Cake

Base:

3oz margarine
4oz caster sugar
6oz self-raising flour
6 tablespoons milk
1 egg

Method:

Cream margarine and sugar. Add flour. Add milk and beaten egg. Stir mixture well and put in well greased flan base.

Topping:

Slice 3-4 cooking apples and arrange on top of sponge mixture.

Crunch:

2oz butter
2oz soft brown sugar
3-4 tablespoons self-raising flour

Method:

Melt butter and soft brown sugar in pan. Remove from heat and add flour until the mixture goes stiff and crumbly. Sprinkle over apples.

Cook in oven gas mark 4/180°C for 45 mins – 1 hour.

Serve with whipped cream.

Betty Williams

Labour-Conway

Betty says there is an interesting history to her contribution, which is of Welsh origin. The recipe was given to Betty in the early 1960s when she was a young socialist, a Labour Party member's mother. She understands it was handed down to her by her grandmother, so it's been around for quite some time.

Welsh Cakes

Ingredients:

8oz self raising flour
Pinch of salt
4oz margarine or butter
2oz caster sugar
2–3oz currants
1 egg (beaten)
1–2 tablespoons cold milk to mix
Quarter teaspoon mixed spice (optional)

Method:

Sift flour, salt (spice) into bowl. Add fat and mix well. Stir in sugar and currants. Mix to stiff paste with beaten egg and milk. Turn on to floured board. Knead lightly. Roll out to quarter inch thick. Cut into rounds with cutter. Cook in frying pan or on a hot plate for about 1–2 minutes per side. Serve warm with caster sugar and butter.

Tony Wright

Labour-Great Yarmouth

Tony, who hails from a windswept Norfolk coastal constituency will stoke up the appetites of readers with these two excellent recipes.

Apple Scone Ring

Ingredients:

8oz plain flour
Half teaspoon salt
2 teaspoon baking powder
2oz margarine
2oz caster sugar
1 medium sized cooking apple, peeled and cored, finely grated
4 tablespoons of milk

Method:

Sieve together flour, salt, baking powder. Rub in margarine. Add the sugar, then the grated apple, and add enough milk to give a soft, but not sticky dough. Turn mixture onto a floured surface and knead lightly. Press out to an 8 inch circle and place on floured baking sheet. Score the scone into 8 pieces. Brush over top with milk and sprinkle with demerara sugar. Bake at 200°C for 20-25 minutes. Cool for ten minutes. Serve with butter.

Chocolate Orange Sponge Cake

Ingredients:

6oz margarine or butter

6oz caster sugar
3 medium sized eggs (beaten)
5oz self-raising flour
2oz cocoa
1 orange (squeezed)

Method:

Cream fat and sugar until light and creamy. Add beaten egg, a small amount at a time, adding a small amount of flour with each addition to prevent curdling. Add about half of the orange juice to mixture and stir in, then sift the rest of the flour on to the mixture and mix in. Divide mixture between two lined 8 inch tins and bake in a pre heated oven at 190°C for approx 30 minutes, until nicely risen. Turn out into a wire tray and leave to cool.

For the filling and topping you will need a 200 gram bar chocolate flavoured cake covering. Break into pieces and place in bowl over a pan of simmering water. Add 1oz margarine, 1 and a half oz icing sugar, and the remaining orange juice. When everything has dissolved to a smooth consistency take off pan. Leave to cool. Place half mixture on one cake, sandwich together. Add remainder to top and decorate as required eg walnuts, cherries etc.

Andy Reed

Labour/Co-Op-Loughborough

Andy says this wonderful cake recipe is a firm favourite for everyone with a sweet tooth. It is also a firm favourite with him as a cook because it's dead easy to make!

Chocolate and Banana Cake

Serves 6-8 Preparation: 15 minutes Cooking time: 1 hour

Ingredients:

2 large ripe bananas
Half teaspoon vanilla essence
6oz margarine
8oz granulated sugar
10oz self raising flour
Pinch of salt
Half teaspoon bicarbonate of soda
3 eggs (size 3) beaten
4oz packet of chocolate chips

Method:

Preheat oven to gas mark 3/325°F/170°C Grease and line 8 inch cake tin. Peel and mash bananas until smooth. Mix together with vanilla essence. Heat margarine and sugar in a pan over a low heat until the sugar dissolves. Remove from the heat. Stir in flour, salt, and bicarbonate of soda. Beat in eggs and mashed banana. Leave to cool. Stir in chocolate chips and spoon into tin. Bake for 1 hour or until skewer inserted in the centre of the cake comes out clean. Leave to cool and decorate with melted chocolate/banana slices half coated in chocolate.

Dr Howard Stoate

Labour-Dartford

Howard says that even a busy MP can find time to make this quick and simple carrot cake. The creamy tanginess of the topping combines perfectly with the healthy wholesomeness of the carrot, leaving a sense of full satisfaction and delight – a truly delicious experience! Even from a GP that takes some swallowing!

Creamy Carrot Cake

Ingredients:

6oz peeled carrots

6oz soft brown sugar or molasses sugar

4oz walnuts or hazelnuts

3oz self raising or wholewheat flour

1 teaspoon cinnamon

1 teaspoon bicarbonate of soda

6 fluid oz sunflower oil

2 large eggs

Topping:

4oz cream cheese

8oz icing sugar

Method:

Using a food processor and metal blade, finely chop carrots and then add nuts and chop on full speed. Change to plastic blade and add all the other ingredients. Blend on full speed for approx 30 seconds. Pour mixture into greased 8 inch square cake tin and bake in centre of oven at Gas Mark 4, 180°C, 350°F, until risen and firm to touch. Leave to cool before turning out.

Topping:

Mix cream cheese with icing sugar and spread over cake. Use nuts to decorate.

Oona King

Labour–Bethnal Green and Bow

Oona has added to the burden of calories that we are undertaking, but obviously with this dish we are going to feel we are in seventh heaven – so go on and try it!

Oona's Divine Chocolate Cake

Ingredients:

300 g of chocolate
150 g butter
150 g sugar
3 free range eggs
180g grated almond pieces

Cooking:

Pre heat oven to 200°C. Melt chocolate slowly in pan. Melt butter separately. When they are both melted add butter to chocolate. Separate eggs and add yolks: mix it all together. Add sugar. Add almonds. Beat egg whites until they are stiff and then add to other ingredients. Put all of it into a greased dish and place in oven for 25 minutes (Check with a spoon to see when it is ready).

Dave Watts

Labour-St Helens North

As this seems such a short recipe and being fatless is also very healthy you can afford to make one than one at a time and freeze, or even just slice and tuck in!

Fatless Fruit Loaf

Ingredients:

1 cup of water
1 cup of brown sugar
12oz mixed fruit
1 egg 2 cups self raising flour
half teaspoon mixed spice

Method:

Put water, sugar and fruit in a pan and bring it to the boil. Cool and add beaten egg, flour, and spice. Bake in a greased 2 lb fruit tin on Gas Mark 5 or 150°C for 1 and a half hours or until cooked.

Tess Kingham

Labour–Gloucester

This recipe uses Fair Trade ingredients. Tess has chosen it not just because it is delicious, but also because, if people use the recipe, farmers and producers in the developing world will benefit more directly from the purchase of the ingredients. All the ingredients should be available from your local Oxfam shop.

Fair Trade Honey Spice Cake
Serves 8

Ingredients:

75g Fair Trade Mexican set honey
250g plain flour
1 teaspoon Fair Trade ground ginger
1 teaspoon Fair Trade ground cinnamon
Half teaspoon ground cloves
75g fair Trade golden caster sugar
Finely grated zest of 1 lemon
Finely grated zest of 1 orange
100g butter
1 egg
1 teaspoon bicarbonate of soda
50g Fair Trade dried apricots blended to a paste

Icing:

100g icing sugar sifted
1 and a half tablespoon lemon juice
2 tablespoons warm water

Method:

Pre heat oven to 160°C/325°F/Gas mark 3 and lightly butter an 18cm square cake tin. Warm the honey in a bowl over a pan of gently simmering water. Sift the flour and spices into a mixing bowl, then add the sugar and fruit zest. Rub the butter into the flour until crumbly. Lightly mix in the egg and honey. In a separate bowl, mix the bicarbonate of soda with 3 tablespoons of cold water until dissolved, then add to the cake mix and beat well. Stir in the apricots and spread the mixture into the tin. Bake in the oven for about 30 minutes. Cool for 10 minutes before turning the cake out onto a cooling rack.

To make the icing – sift the icing sugar into a bowl. Add the water and lemon juice and mix well until blended. Pour the icing over the cake and leave for a short time to set.

Jenny Jones

Labour-Wolverhampton South West

Last orders are being called, for here is the one and only drink recipe that was submitted. From the numerous bars in Westminster where intrigue and deals are supposed to emanate we thought MPs might have a tasty array of tipsy beverages at their fingertips – political cocktails perhaps? (or maybe that is another book!)

Jenny explains that recipes for Damson Gin are not uncommon, but the one she has sent in is an old family recipe handed down through three generations of her mother's family. It is foolproof (as well as being high percentage proof!) with the secret being in allowing the sugar to dissolve into the damson juice before adding the alcohol. Jenny would not normally part with the recipe but as she is a great cat lover too she says she'd do just about anything for cats!

Damson Gin

Ingredients:

1lb of damsons
(must be ripe and perfect, no bruises or overripe)

3oz of white sugar (preferably caster sugar)

1 and a half pints of gin

Method:

Remove stalks from damsons, wipe clean, and prick fruit with plastic or wooden toothpicks (not metal) about half a dozen times to get the juice flowing from the fruit. Pack the damsons into a glass jar and add sugar. Screw down the top and shake the jar a couple of times to ensure the sugar coats the fruit. Leave until the sugar has dissolved (this can take a day or two) Add the gin and shake the jar. Put the jar in a dark and cool place and invert the jar each day for about 2 months. After two months strain the fruit through a plastic sieve and put the damson gin in a bottle and cork. The gin can be drunk straight away but it definitely improves with keeping for a few months before drinking. The 'drunken' damsons are also delicious to eat, and are particularly good with either cream or Greek yoghurt. As they have been steeped in alcohol the damsons will keep for some time in the fridge.